Brian Ming

FOREWORD BY BOB SORGE

14418 Miller Ave. Unit K
Fontana, CA 92336
www.website-url.com

Edited by Edie Mourey (www.furrowpress.com).

ISBN-13: 978-1537154930

ISBN-10: 1537154931

Contents

When I think about the attributes described in this book, I can't think of anyone who exemplifies the secret heart of God more than my mother. As a child, I remember countless hours of hearing her pray, worship, and seek the heart of God. Growing up, I hoped for a fraction of that type of intimacy with Jesus. Now as an adult, as I watched her care for my aged father, I have newfound respect for seeing the heart of God in action. In the latter part of my Dad's life, in loving and selfless sacrifice, I can only speak to the fruit of which I saw and respond accordingly, "Well done." I love you, Mom!

FOREWORD

Secret of Stories

MY FRIENDSHIP WITH Brian Ming is long and very meaningful to me personally. We have enjoyed ministering and fellowshipping together through the years, and I've been blessed by his songwriting and worship ministry. The reach of his gift is now extending to writing. And it's my honor and privilege to partner with Him again by writing this foreword.

Stories are powerful. In this book, Brian Ming harnesses the power of story to illustrate secrets in God's heart that He wants to make known to us.

The reason stories are powerful is because, when we tell a story, others find themselves in the story and gain courage and understanding for their own journey. As you follow Brian's storytelling, the same is likely to happen for you. You're probably going to find that, as God's heart is revealed for others, His secret desires for your life will also be identified.

Jesus told stories. In fact, the Bible is chock-full of stories. Stories help truths lodge permanently in our memory banks. They're the best way to make a point.

This is why your whole life is a story. God is making of your life a point that will be a legacy for others. He writes great stories. When Paul called you "an epistle of Christ" (2 Cor 3:3), he meant your life is a story that is being crafted by the Alpha and Omega—the consummate Author—Jesus Christ.

Furthermore, within the broad strokes of your life, He writes many smaller vignettes or stories that end up inspiring and helping others. Let me illustrate with the apostle Paul.

When Paul (then named Saul) was traveling the road to Damascus, it's as though Jesus said to him, "Buckle up, I'm about to give you a good story." He knocked Paul to the ground, showed Himself to him, blinded him, interrogated him, gave him a new life calling, and then healed him. The whole story was so dramatic!

And when you follow Paul's ministry in the book of Acts, you find him telling this experience over and over again. Why? Because of the power that resided in that story.

Paul's Damascus road story had the kind of power on it that enabled those who could not grasp the message of the gospel to wrap their fingers around something in the Kingdom and lay hold of their eternal destiny. Where gospel principles did not penetrate, the dazzling screenplay of a true episode could pierce the darkness and reach a needy heart.

God still does the same today. He writes stories with our lives that have such power on them that seekers can get a handle on the meaning of the gospel. A way is made for those who could not otherwise find their way.

What we need today, more than ever, are men and women with stories in God that are so compelling that they shift eternal destinies.

It's interesting to follow how Paul used his testimony. Whenever he found himself in front of a particularly tough crowd, he would pull out his Damascus road story. Why? Because it had power on it to defuse animosity and win the hearts of skeptics.

May Jesus write a Damascus-caliber story with your life. May He unfold the secrets that will give the story impact and relevance. May the secrets in this book's stories help you cooperate with His purposes until He's finished with every chapter of your life.

BOB SORGE
Oasis House, Kansas City, MO
August 2017

INTRODUCTION

Secret Heart of God

AT JUST UNDER A HUNDRED and fifty pages, some might think I wrote this book in a matter of months or possibly a year—tops. The truth is, it's taken me two decades.

Why so long? What have I been doing all that time?

For twenty years, God and I have been playing a mysterious and awe-filled game of hide-and-seek. Unlike the game I played as a child, God's version had a whole different set of rules. In fact, until I learned His rules—and decided to play on His terms—I couldn't participate. Neither could I seem to find Him.

The popular song "Pieces" by Amanda Cook helps describe my journey. Referring to God, it says:

"You don't give your heart in pieces. You don't hide yourself to tease us."[1]

I've learned the second line of that song is true, and I'll take it one step further. *When God hides Himself, He's not trying to provoke or frustrate us. He's extending an invitation to come search for Him.* It's in the midst of the chase that God reveals life-transforming secrets well worth the effort, struggle, and years of searching and waiting. And in the end, we receive what we set out to do: We find Him!

Surprisingly, during my game of hide-and-seek with God, I also discovered Satan has secrets, planted like hidden landmines and meant for my destruction. When God began to point out these dangers, I remember thinking: *Oh, thank You, Lord, for bringing this to my attention. These are topics many people need to hear about.* Little did I know at the time that God was not the least bit worried about changing other people—He was trying to get through to me.

In years of pastoral counseling, I found it tragic how, many times, people don't discover their hidden flaws until it's too late. I've counseled men whose wives want nothing more to do with them. They often say, "I didn't know what was wrong. Now that I do, I would do anything to go back and fix my mistakes." Unfortunately, by the time they discovered Satan's destructive secrets, their lives, marriages, or ministries had been destroyed.

In his book, *The Fire of His Holiness,* Sergio Scataglini wrote:

"God is only comfortable when we are uncomfortable."[2]

As you read through *Secret Heart of God*, I'll forewarn you, this book is not about comfort. Neither is this book going to tell you things you want to hear—but things you probably need to hear. The reason? To spur you on towards God's heart as well as warn you about Satan's destructive landmines during your journey.

God has extended an invitation to play hide-and-seek with Him. Should you choose to participate, I'm confident you'll find the secret heart of God is a deep well far beyond anything that can be dreamed about or imagined. Satan looms with secret tactics meant to derail you from knowing and experiencing the truth about God's heart. I'd like to say the journey is safe—and easy. But that would be a lie. Although God is compassionate and loving, I've also discovered, at times He is a roaring lion. The nuances of His heart are as vast as He is magnificent.

The stage is set. The game is about to begin. With childlike faith, why not say, "Ready or not, here I come!"

CHAPTER 1

Secret of One

SECRETS ARE MEANT to be discovered. You don't keep secrets forever; they are revealed in their due time.

God has secrets. Found deep in His heart, these treasures are so valuable He graciously hides them from plain sight—fingers crossed—quietly waiting for those willing to come and search for them. Although available to all, few find them.

Tough Journey

My family, some friends, and I moved halfway across the country to plant a church. You can imagine the emotions I was feeling. Or maybe you can't. I know I had never experienced the pressure of having relocated eleven people, all trusting in the plan I'd received from God to start Worship Central Church. We named the church accordingly because of my background as a worship leader and emphasis on being a church that valued God's presence. Our vision was simple: Worship Central Church—*Where worship is central in everyday life*. As we pulled into North San Diego County, our faith was high and we couldn't be more excited.

Anyone who has ever planted a church knows it's hard work. I've heard similar reports from many who have said, "It was the hardest thing I've ever done." We soon learned just how hard, as some of the funding unexpectedly fell through in the beginning stages. Yet, at the same time, we also saw miracles seeming to confirm God's favor in what we were doing—such as reaching our first several people who started attending our home Bible study and, shortly after, finding a building to meet in on Sunday nights.

In December, just six months into our journey, things were extremely tight financially. So tight, in fact, I was already having thoughts of giving up. One night I vented to my wife, "Why would God send us to such an expensive place to live and then allow a big portion of our funding to get pulled? I just don't understand." Deep down, however, I had a strong sense we were where God wanted us. Our Sunday night meetings had grown to over thirty with many of those in attendance making commitments to Christ for the first time.

Even in the growth, I remember thinking: *How will we make it financially? We need more funding.* I didn't voice it, but on many occasions, I wondered: *Did I miss it?* I couldn't deny I'd heard from God—that I knew for sure. And yet, one thought lingered: *Perhaps I missed the timing.*

Through the years, I'd heard people I trust say, "Sometimes we get God's plan right, but miss His timing." When Christmas time rolled around and we had no extra money to buy presents for our kids, I thought that was exactly what happened.

Confirmation

Two things transpired in January that changed my thinking and confirmed we were on the right path. First, a great church adopted us and started supporting us monthly, which drastically changed our financial picture. Second, on Sunday evening, January 10, I gave a call for salvation and three people raised their hands, one of whom was a young marine named Charlie. He'd been attending over the previous few months.

After the service, I made a point to find Charlie and congratulate him. Patting him on the back, I said, "I'm so happy you made the decision to follow Christ. Get ready for an amazing ride. We're here to help you."

Charlie smiled and kind of pulled me off to the side saying, "Yeah, I've been thinking about it and asking Jeff [the marine who had invited him] a lot of questions. And, I finally decided to do it." He went on to say something sort of confusing, "I'm glad I did, but I have a secret I need to tell you. I'm not ready to tell you yet, but I will."

I was kind of taken aback, "Uh, well...okay," I said, searching for a response. "Well, I'd love to hear it, so let me know when you're ready. I'd recommend sooner rather than later, okay?"

"Maybe next week," Charlie said.

I didn't press any further, but replied, "Okay, maybe next week then."

That night we went home thrilled by the response—especially for Charlie. Although I had no idea what he meant by the strange secret, I sensed his commitment to follow Christ was genuine. He'd taken his time and researched, asked Jeff questions, and finally reached a decision. Although things were still hard on several fronts, we were once again reminded God was at work.

The following week, I saw Charlie arrive early as usual and greeted him. What he said about the secret had been eating at me all week. I shook his hand and joked, "Hey Charlie, you ready to tell me that secret—I'm curious, you know?"

He laughed and replied, "Yeah, I'm ready. I'll tell you after the meeting tonight."

"Deal," I said, and traipsed off to get ready for worship. I had no idea how this night would change my perspective forever.

Charlie's Secret

I stood in a back room alone with Charlie who usually maintained a pleasant demeanor. Not anymore. He was nervous, and I sensed he was still hesitant to tell me his secret.

"Hey, it's okay, Charlie," I reaffirmed. "I'm here to support you, no matter what kind of secret you have."

With his head down, he whispered, "I was going to commit suicide."

I gulped, wondering if I'd heard right.

He looked up at me eyeball to eyeball and said, "When I say I was going to commit suicide—I really mean it. I had a spot picked out on the Coronado Bridge, a date, and a time I was going to do it."

I didn't know what to say. I wasn't ready for that.

Charlie stammered, lost for the right words, but continued, "I...you know...had just lost all hope. I really had nothing to live for. I thought being in the military would give me a purpose, but found it to be empty and shallow.

And for whatever reason, the thought of suicide consumed me. It was all I could think about."

He's serious, I shook my head as the weight of his words sank in.

"On the morning I planned to do it, I received a text from Jeff asking me if I wanted to go to this new church he was attending on Sunday nights. I thought about it and decided to put off my plans until the following Sunday and said yes." Charlie's countenance seemed to change, and he smiled. "That was my first Sunday at Worship Central and, obviously, not my last."

"Well, I'm glad you made the choice to come," I said, almost breathing for the first time since he'd started.

"Me too," Charlie said, now beaming from ear to ear. "I was nervous to tell you because it was embarrassing. But, Jeff encouraged me to. And just so you know, now that Jesus has become a part of my life, suicide is the last thing on my mind."

Tears filled my eyes at Charlie's words, and it was all I could do to hold it together. Later that night, however, when I told my wife, all the emotions came out, and I cried hard. We both did. As we sat in the kitchen rejoicing over the amazing story, I finally shared with her how discouraged I'd been feeling. I also admitted how, through the difficulty, I'd been wondering if I'd missed God's timing.

She went on to say, "If we wouldn't have moved when we did, Charlie might have gone through with his plans. God knew we were supposed to be here—for Charlie."

Had we come for one—for Charlie? Was she right? My heart ached for having doubted God's plan during times of hardship. *How could we have known our being here and obeying His voice was a matter of life and death—literally life and not death—for Charlie?*

After that night, no longer did I doubt God's timing. He made it abundantly clear—in a way only He can—that we were hearing His voice clearly and fulfilling His mandate obediently.

Prodigal Brother

My experience with Charlie has forever changed my perspective on God's love. Here's the raw facts: Multiplied thousands of dollars were spent, eleven people were relocated hundreds of miles, and we all endured incredible hardship to, if nothing else, reach one: Charlie. What a beautiful picture of the Good Shepherd leaving the ninety-nine to go after the one (see Matt 18:12).

Although God's love for one is found throughout Scripture, there's no more breathtaking view than the story of the prodigal son. Unparalleled is the imagery of a loving father waiting patiently, desperately watching, and vehemently yearning for his son's return from folly. The climax occurs when the wayward son, expecting to return as a servant, falls into his father's arms and is welcomed back into the household as a son. Magnificent!

As touching as the father's embrace is when his son returns, I find the subplot of the story far more intriguing.

Before we go any further, it is important to note the family dynamics. Although fictional, Jesus portrayed a typical wealthy Jewish family. This close-knit household would have worked together, ate every meal together, and likely slept in the same room or in very close proximity. Think about Joseph and the sons of Israel for a minute. All the squabbling, jealousy, horseplay, and overall drama that existed paints a fairly accurate picture of the family Jesus described.

After the prodigal returns, act two of the story begins with the introduction of the lost son's older brother. Upon arriving home from a long day's work, the older brother hears music, dancing, and, after asking a servant, learns the fattened calf has been slaughtered. He can't believe his ears. Killing the beast (likely raised for a wedding ceremony or special occasion) is evidence of how significant the father viewed the prodigal's return. The older brother is so furious he refuses to attend the celebration; instead, he stews outside.

Perhaps the older brother raised the fattened calf and had a special attachment of some kind. Maybe he hoped the calf might be slaughtered in honor of his wedding. Based on his response, another theory comes to mind that might be more accurate. I wonder if the older brother, like Judas Iscariot, who scorned the sinful woman's extravagant use of oil on Jesus' feet, said in his heart: *What a waste of such a costly possession.* Although Judas's response made it appear he had a deep desire to help the poor, we know with certainty something entirely different was going on in his heart (see John 12:6).

A Christian counselor I know made a startling statement I've never forgotten:

"When I counsel people, I rarely get an honest take on their situation. Most of the time, I get the reality they want me to see, and, unfortunately, that's the reality they end up living with. Many times, they are completely blinded to the truth—especially the truth about themselves."

This not only describes Judas's take on the woman who anointed Jesus' feet, but also the reaction of the prodigal's brother. What was really going on that made him so upset?

When the father finds him outside and encourages him to attend the party, he snaps, "When this son of yours comes home after squandering your money with prostitutes, you kill the fattened calf" (Luke 15:30). As with Judas, although correct in his assessment, there is something else going on within his heart. Further justifying his disdain, he complains, "Look! All these years I've been slaving for you and never disobeyed your orders. Yet you never gave me even a young goat so I could celebrate with my friends" (Luke 15:29).

I wonder if Judas—not feeling the same closeness with Jesus as Peter, James, and John—felt the same kind of resentment as the older brother? It's uncertain. Yet, in this telling statement, we learn much about the older brother's icy reaction. Surprisingly, the reason had nothing to do with his younger brother and everything to do with the way he viewed his father's feelings for him.

In my mind, I can't help but question: *Who was the real prodigal in this story?* It appears there was not one—but two. The prodigal son is obvious; the other, often overlooked, is what, from now on, I'll call the *prodigal brother.*

Love Surpassing Knowledge

Maybe you can relate to my upbringing. Without ever being communicated in these plain terms, I was led to believe the following theology: Try all you want, but in the end, you will never *ever* understand the depth of God's love. Scripture references such as, "how wide and long and high and deep is the love of Christ" (Eph 3:18) were used to discourage any attempt to fully grasp the overwhelming love of our heavenly Father.

It wasn't until I began to study God's heart I discovered His intense desire to reveal the mystery of His love. The aforementioned passage doesn't discourage us from trying to understand God's love but is an invitation from God to, in fact, know and grasp it:

> *And I pray that you, being rooted and established in love, may have power, together with all the Lord's holy people, to grasp how wide and long and high and deep is the love of Christ, and to know this love that surpasses knowledge—that you may be filled to the measure of all the fullness of God. (Eph 3:18-19)*

In this passage, I don't see God at all communicating, "Give it a try and, try as you may, you'll never understand it." I see God saying just the opposite with terms like *be rooted*, *established,* and *grasp.* These tell me He wants me to know His incredible love.

In the middle of this passage, we also learn an important key to understanding God's love: "know this love that surpasses knowledge" (v. 19). The truth is, you can't understand it with knowledge alone. Why? Because God's love for you and me (wide, long, high, and deep as it is) *surpasses* knowledge! I've heard it said,

---

"The key to understanding God's love is about eighteen inches—the span between one's mind and one's heart."

Perhaps this is why the prodigal brother was living in a household of exceedingly great love and didn't know it.

I Loved You the Same

It was a normal day when I knelt at the edge of my bed praying. For months God had been wrestling with me about understanding His love. After discovering the truth about His love surpassing knowledge, I asked the Lord, "Okay, God, if I can't understand it with my head, then show me—in a way only You can—how much You love me." Then I put my head in my hands and waited.

A few minutes later, in the silence, my mind flashed to a dreadful time just after my graduation from high school when I was eighteen years old. My friends, knowing I'd never consumed alcohol, took me out with the intention to get the preacher's kid drunk. I'm embarrassed to say, before the night was through, I'd consented to taking over a dozen shots of tequila. By the fifth or sixth shot, I don't remember anything, but supposedly, they took me home and threw me on my bed because I had passed out.

In the middle of the night, I rolled off the bed, and the first thing I remember is waking up in a pool of my own vomit. My mom knelt over me crying out of obvious concern and ended up having to hand-bathe me. Needless to say, it was not my most shining moment.

After reliving the horrific memory, I kind of shook my head out of the daydream and thought: *That was definitely one of my all-time lows.*

Thinking I'd let my mind wander (as I sometimes do in prayer), I refocused my attention and again asked the Lord, "I'm serious. Show me how much you love me. I really want to know."

Once again, I grew quiet and listened for His voice, not exactly sure what I was expecting to hear. A few minutes later, my mind flashed to another time in my life—about ten years later—when I'd taken a brave step to fast from solid food for forty days and nights. On day forty, after almost six weeks without a bite of food, I had an incredible encounter with God at a conference I was attending.

As I relived the memory, I reminisced: *We were super tight back then, Lord. I remember how amazing that forty-day journey was.* And that's when I heard God's voice say something I'll never forget. Like my experience with hearing Charlie's secret, it sent shockwaves through my mind. Imagine my surprise when God said, "Don't you realize, Brian, I loved you exactly the same on both those days? My love for you never changed."

As I pictured myself drunk on the floor in stark contrast with how I was on day forty of my fast, tears came to my eyes. The truth of that reality exploded in my head like a volcanic eruption. "But how? Why? How could You possibly love me the same?" I stammered. While my mind spun uncontrollably, my heart seemed to settle peacefully within my chest. The more I meditated on it, the more I realized God had answered my prayer more profoundly than I could have imagined.

In that moment, *I realized my perception of God's love stemmed from my ability to perform well rather than His ability to love well.* Wow, what a change in thinking!

Secret of One

Maybe you are like I was and believe if you perform well today, God must love you more. Just as faulty is thinking your poor performance today means He loves you less. The hardest reality to grasp of all, perhaps, is that God's love for you today is no more or no less than His love for you tomorrow, or a hundred or a million years from now. When God said, "I have loved you with an everlasting love" (Jer 31:3), and "I the Lord do not change" (Mal 3:6), He actually meant it. If that's true, the father's love for the prodigal was the same on the day he left as on the day he returned, and every day in between—including the time the son spent in the pig pen.

If the father's love was so extravagant, what was the prodigal brother's problem? Surely, he must have known how much he was loved? Yet, while his brother received the fattened calf, he responds, "you never gave me even a young goat so I could celebrate with my friends" (v. 30).

There are two different kinds of love (and two different perspectives) being identified here: a skinny goat kind of love (which the prodigal brother felt he deserved) and a fattened calf type of love (which the prodigal son felt he didn't deserve). Interestingly, both sons' pretenses are wrong. Both perspectives express an absence of the secret heart of God.

Here's my interpretation of what the prodigal brother was saying: "Dad, for years I've been a hardworking son, and, based on my performance, I've failed because you haven't given me what I want." Let me say it another way: "Dad, no matter what I do or don't do, it'll never be good enough to truly deserve your favor and admiration."

Let me put myself in the story: "God, I know You love Charlie so much so, You sent me and a whole team from halfway across the country on a rescue mission. But I on the other hand...well, when it comes to me, that's another story."

Maybe like me, you've held to the knowledge that God loves everybody—especially people like Charlie. That's easy to grasp. Believing that God solely loves *you* may be more of a stretch.

In all this, where do we find the secret heart of God? Is it God's love for the prodigal son, or is it God's love for the prodigal brother? Is it God's love for Charlie or God's love for me? The answer to all these questions is *yes!* The father loved the older brother every bit as much as he loved the younger. The tragedy is, while he had full access to his father's love and affection, the prodigal brother didn't believe it. I know I didn't. Not until I discovered the secret of one.

I'm the one God loves.

How amazing that, in my experience of reaching Charlie, I discovered how much God loves *me*. I was a prodigal brother, always feeling the need to prove myself. Always feeling unworthy based on my poor performance. And all along, He's been crazy about me!

As God sometimes does, He gave me this song to help so I could declare the truth about His love in worship.

I'm the One

I'm the one my Savior loves
I'm the reason that He came
Of the hundred minus one
I'm the one He chose to save
I'm the one, the one my Savior loves
The one He came to save
Because my heart was lost
I'm the one, the one my Savior loves
The reason that He gave
His life upon a cross

Even as I sang it for the first time, as wrong as it sounded, I desperately wanted to believe it was true. John the apostle certainly believed it. In fact, from his writings, we learn who God is: "God is love" (1 John 4:16).

You notice John doesn't say, "God has love," or even, "God loves." John makes an important distinction: "God *is* love." Love is not what God does; it's who He is!

A few verses later, John teaches us about our capacity to love based on one important reality: "We love because He first loved us" (1 John 4:19). Before we were born, took a breath, sinned or repented of that sin, God *first* loved us.

Later in John's Revelation, he makes what I consider the most startling statement in all of Scripture revealing when, in God's mind, He made the decision to send His beloved Son. John describes Jesus as "the Lamb slain from the foundation of the world" (Rev 13:8). Think about how staggering a statement this is. Before our existence and before the world was formed, God *first* loved us—and chose to be our sacrificial lamb.

John not only believed in this love that surpasses knowledge, he let it change who he was. Often, John described himself as the disciple whom Jesus loved (see John 20:8; John 21:20). How could he make such an audacious statement? It's simple. John had discovered the secret of one. Yes, he knew God loved everyone—all the disciples—and yet, John was the one disciple Jesus loved.

I find it interesting how, at the Last Supper, while Peter and the other disciples confidently vowed to die for Jesus, here was John's posture: "Now there was leaning on Jesus' bosom one of His disciples, whom Jesus loved" (John 13:23 NKJV). Twenty-four hours later, while all the other disciples fled and hid, John was the only courageous one to show his face at Jesus' crucifixion. John stood and watched—heartbroken—comforting Mary, the

Lord's mother. And before the end, Jesus entrusted her to John as her caregiver. Why? Jesus looked down from the cross and saw someone who could *receive* love from God and, because of that fact, had great capacity to *show* love to others.

Oh, how powerful the secret of one is. If you dare to believe it, this single revelation of God's love for everyone, but solely for you, will radically change your walk. The kid's song, "Jesus Loves Me," is actually true. Who knew? I wonder why, as adults, we stopped singing and believing it?

CHAPTER 2

Secret of I

I REMEMBER HOW difficult making the transition from the role of worship leader to pastor was. I'd been in various leadership positions and on stages in front of crowds of thousands for years. In our first service at Worship Central Church, we literally had more people in the band on stage than in the crowd.

At the same time God was teaching me the secret of one, He was also examining my heart. He began to challenge me through my thoughts: *Am I okay ministering to the one? Was moving all the way across the country, if for no other reason but to reach Charlie, okay with me?* As much as I said *yes,* I sensed a hesitation that left me wondering.

It reminded me of a time earlier in my ministry when I had a strong desire to produce a worship album. At one point, someone stepped forward and said he would help me produce it. Around the same time, another person said he would help me pay for it. You can imagine how excited I was. I assumed God was putting all the pieces together so that my worship could get out to the masses.

At the climax of this opportunity, I remember God asking me in prayer one day: "Why do you want to make a worship album?" I immediately thought of all the spiritual reasons why the world needed my worship album and disregarded His question.

I've discovered when God asks you a question He's not seeking information. Think about when Adam and Eve were hiding in the garden after they sinned. As He often did, God showed up in the cool of the day and yelled out, "Adam! Eve! Where are you?" (see Gen 3:8-9). This is quite comical since the all-knowing God—Creator of the universe—knew full well of their location.

So I wonder, why would God call out to them? And even after they came out from hiding, why would He ask, "Have you been eating from the tree I told you not to?"

The answer is simple. Although God knew they'd been deceived by Satan, they didn't know it. Instead, they hid, covering themselves with leaves.

God has a distinct way of getting our attention. One of my college instructors, Edmund Janzen, made this statement:

"Many times in the American church, we don't change until we hurt enough that we have to."

This statement certainly rang true for me as I ignored God's question until all the doors for the worship album slammed shut.

Utterly deflated, my mind defaulted to one place: God's question—"Why do you want to make a worship album?" I decided to answer and proceeded in giving Him all kinds of "spiritual-sounding" reasons. You know the kind I mean, where you act like a child in Sunday school class trying to impress your Sunday school teacher. After a while, though I tried hard to look good, I realized I couldn't hide the intents of my heart. "I want to show off how well I can sing, and I want people to know what a great songwriter I am." There. I said it. Ouch! That hurts to admit.

Looking back at my answer, I see four "I's" staring at me. It's what I've come to call the *I factor.*

The I Factor

When I was thirteen years old, I decided to join the high school basketball team. Now let me give you a little scenario of my physical stature at age thirteen. I was a late bloomer, standing five feet and two inches tall with a size thirteen tennis shoe. My brothers told me, if I'd ever grow into my feet, I'd be six feet and seven inches, playing at a major university on a full-ride scholarship.

On top of my being vertically challenged and having huge feet, I was also about thirty pounds overweight. Talk about clumsy. I think I spent half of the first week of tryouts on the ground, tripping over my own feet. They say white men can't jump. I'm not sure if that's true, but I can tell you that short chubby white boys with big feet can't jump. While most guys were stretching to touch the rim, I was stretching to touch the bottom of the net.

By some miracle (or maybe because the coach felt sorry for me), I made the basketball team. I remember a pep talk one night before a game. "Men, there is no 'I' in 'team,'" Coach Wells told us. Not only was I a terrible basketball player, I was also pretty dense. I had no idea why the letter *I* not being in the word *team* could win us the game. *Oh well*, I thought, *I have a lot of time to think about it on the bench during the game.*

Finally, it hit me in the second quarter. *No "I" in "team"—duh!* He meant we were to play as a team and not as individuals—*okay, I get it.*

There may be no "I" in the word "team," but the letter *I* falls right smack dab in the middle of the word *pride.*

Although Satan has worked overtime to keep the *I* in *pride* hidden, Scripture has a great deal to say about it. The wise Solomon said, "A man's pride shall bring him low: but honor shall uphold the humble in spirit" (Prov 29:23), and, "Pride goes before destruction, and a haughty spirit before a fall" (Prov 16:18). Satan's secret of I sounds dangerous, but what is it? And more importantly, where does it come from?

Every child has asked this question, "Mommy, where does that come from?" All the way from a small scoop of ice cream to a soaring skyscraper, kids just have to know, "Where did it come from?"

Some things are easy to explain: "Ice cream? Well, honey, we get milk from a cow. We purify it, add sugar, shake it up, freeze it, and *voilà*—we have ice cream!" Other things are more difficult. "A skyscraper? Well, honey, it starts with a solid foundation. You dig a big hole, put pipes for plumbing, put in all the electrical, pour the concrete, and then you're ready to start building."

"Uh, Mommy?"

"Yes, dear."

"What's a solid fundignation?"

Mom tries not to grin too widely and replies, "You'll understand when you're older—it's just a big building!"

"But Mommy, where did it come from?"

Unless you're a scientist, somewhere along the line, most people give up trying to figure out, "Where did it come from?" I find this dangerous when it comes to our own character issues. At some point, in frustration to a part of our nature we don't like, we give up and exclaim, "This is just the way I am!" When it comes to the secret of I issue we all face, can we become like little children again and ask, "Where did it come from?"

Satan's secret of I begins mentally. It's like the story of little Johnny who is running around in the doctor's office. When other patients begin to get annoyed, his mother tells him to sit down and be quiet. Johnny disregards his mother's correction and keeps playing. His mother tells him again in a firmer tone, "Johnny, I said to sit down!"

Johnny again ignores his mother and continues on. Finally, in frustration, his mother gets up and forces him into the chair. Knowing he's lost the battle, Johnny looks sternly at his mom and says, "I may be sitting down on the outside, but, on the inside, I'm standing up!"

The secret of I begins on the inside. It buries itself until someone steps too close. It won't surface until the circumstances force you to evaluate your motives by requiring radical submission to God's will. It's what surfaced when God asked me why I wanted to make a worship album. The secret of I not only affects what we do, but also motivates what we do.

Satan's Best Kept Secret

In war, any general will tell you the element of surprise is a very powerful tactic used to conquer the enemy. It can, in itself, be the difference between victory and defeat. Such was the case in World War II, when the United

States surprised the world by dropping its secret weapon—the atomic bomb—on the cities of Hiroshima and Nagasaki. At the end of these acts of offense, not only were one-hundred and twenty thousand dead, but the war was over.

Satan has secrets. Whereas God's secrets lead to abundant life, Satan's secrets lead to death. Throughout the ages, those deceived by his secret tactics discover, like stepping on a hidden landmine, it's too late. It's game over; the trap is sprung, and destruction comes quickly.

For most of my teenage and young adult life, I fell prey to Satan's secret tactics. Being molested as a child thrust me into a fleshly existence only those who have experienced such abuse can fully understand. Because of the abuse I experienced, I'm sad to admit, I was held in bondage by one addiction after another for many years.

Walking through those difficult times, I not only learned the power of Satan's secrets, but how to identify the difference between roots and weeds. Weeds are easily identified. For instance, if a believer is cheating the time clock at work, eventually, if yielded to the Holy Spirit, he begins to feel convicted and think: *I really should stay until the end of my shift*. Without much thought, the decision is made to change his behavior. Instead of leaving work early, he decides to sit down and have a cup of coffee until the shift is officially over. Problem solved, right? Not exactly!

Changing his behavior only removes the weeds without dealing with the roots. Without knowing it, he's replaced one sin for another, and as much as he feels better for "putting in the time," he misses the hidden issue: laziness.

When the Holy Spirit tries to point out the root to him, he thinks: *Laziness? It couldn't possibly be? I want to work. I'm a worker!* Meanwhile, Satan relishes in the secret he's hidden under the surface of the man's heart and continues to hold the worker in bondage. Like Eve in the garden, without knowing it, he is deceived.

As I unveil Satan's best kept secret, try to keep an open mind. Don't disregard the destruction his tactic can do. When it's mentioned, people automatically think: *I don't need to hear about that; that's not an issue in my life.* If you're thinking that, or have ever thought it, chances are this secret has already been unleashed, and you don't even know it. That's what I discovered, anyway, when I tried to ignore God's questioning me about the worship album.

In *The Purpose Driven Life*, a book that has sold over thirty million copies worldwide, Rick Warren starts with this statement:

"It's not about you."[3]

The premise of the book is to discover God's divine purpose for one's life, thus the title. It's interesting that in order to do so, he starts by identifying the problem: *you (and me).*

The Root of All Sin

Knowing the root of a problem is necessary to address the problem. Wouldn't it be wonderful to know the true cause of cancer? Study after study has tried to determine the physical cause of getting cancer. We know if you are a smoker, it is more likely you will get lung cancer. Many smokers live long and full lives, however, and are free from cancer. Smoking is a condition that enhances whatever is causing cancer—but it's not the cause.

We all know sin is bad. We know that sin separates us from God and ultimately leads to death. We all understand the *effects* of sin. But what is the *cause* of sin?

Unlike cancer, we know the cause of sin. Did you know that the first act of sin—ever—was pride? That's right. Before Adam and Eve walked the earth, a few Old Testament prophets gave us a glimpse at where sin came from.

> *You were the seal of perfection, full of wisdom and perfect in beauty. You were in Eden, the garden of God; every precious stone adorned you: carnelian, chrysolite and emerald, topaz, onyx and jasper, lapis lazuli, turquoise and beryl. Your settings and mountings were made of gold; on the day you were created they were prepared. You were anointed as a guardian cherub, for so I ordained you. You were on the holy mount of God; you walked among the fiery stones. You were blameless in your ways from the day you were created till wickedness was found in you. Through your widespread trade you were filled with violence, and you sinned. So I drove you in disgrace from the mount of God, and I expelled you, guardian cherub, from among the fiery stones. Your heart became proud on account of your beauty, and you corrupted your wisdom because of your splendor. (Ezek 28:12-17)*

The word *proud* here comes from the Hebrew word *gabahh* (gaw-bah'). It means to soar, be lofty, be haughty, exalt, be (make) higher, lift up, mount up, be proud, raise up to great heights, upward.

In this passage, we learn Lucifer was created to perfection. He was more beautiful than any other angel. His body was crafted with the sole purpose of giving glory to God. In today's terms, he was the worship leader of heaven and of the band of musicians.

The New King James Version reads: "The workmanship of your timbrels and pipes was prepared for you on the day you were created" (Ezek 28:13). With musical instruments literally built into Lucifer's body, he must have been quite a sight to behold.

For a period of time, he was blameless in all his ways. But, then, something changed; his heart became proud. We have no explanation as to why the change occurred, but it is beyond a doubt that something in Lucifer's nature began to look away from God and focus upon himself. Isaiah's account gives us another look at his dangerous secret mind shift.

> *How you have fallen from heaven, O morning star, son of the dawn! You have been cast down to the earth, you who once laid low the nations! You said in your heart, "I will ascend to heaven; I will raise my throne above the stars of God; I will sit enthroned on the mount of assembly, on the utmost heights of the sacred mountain. I will ascend above the tops of the clouds; I will make myself like the most High." (Isa 14:12-14)*

Five times, Lucifer exclaimed, "I will," each time elevating himself a little higher, until finally the motivation of his heart was made known. Each "I will" revealed more and more of the root issue—"I will make myself like the most High." How deceived Lucifer had become. It's interesting to note that, in the garden, when the serpent (Lucifer) gave Eve the forbidden fruit, he tempted her with the same idea: "Come on, eat this fruit and you will be like God, knowing good and evil. Don't you want to be like God?" (see Gen 3:4).

Whenever I've heard this text taught, I assumed Lucifer audibly said, "I will be like God." Not so. It states, "he said in his heart" (v. 13).

We cannot assume just because we don't make such claims aloud there's no pride in our hearts. Solomon so eloquently taught, "For as he thinks in his heart, so is he" (Prov 23:7 KJV).

To human knowledge, this was the first account of sin—the first transgression by creation against the Creator. Thus, it could be said the root of all sin is pride. Pride is what caused Lucifer to fall. Pride caused Eve to say, "God, I'm going to disregard what You told me because the fruit is 'good for food and pleasing to the eye, and also desirable for gaining wisdom'" (Gen 3:6).

Any sin you can think of can be traced back to pride. Lust: *I like that*. Jealousy: *I want what you have*. Greed: *I want more and more*. Sin: *I'm doing it. It feels good. I, I, I!*

Pride is selfish and leads to sin. Maybe that's why both *pride* and *sin* have *I* right in the middle of them.

What a stark contrast is God's secret of one and Satan's secret of I. Satan works overtime to keep our ulterior motives hidden. Meanwhile, God is so crazy in love with us, He'll walk through the garden yelling our names, "Adam! Eve! Brian! Where are you?" to get our attention. In Adam and Eve's case, after they came out from hiding, God took their meager attempt at covering themselves (with leaves) and, many believe, offered a blood sacrifice, covering them properly (see Gen 3:21).

Even as far back as the beginning, the secret of God's heart for one was evident. Several millennia later, when Satan's secret of I had ruled for ages, it was the power of one—God's one and only Son—who shattered pride and sin forever!

CHAPTER 3

Secret of Blind Trust

MOST CHRISTIANS CAN agree that God has an orchestrated plan for every believer's life. We all have a destiny. Peter's destiny was to preach the gospel to the Jews. Paul's destiny was to preach the gospel to the Gentiles. If you know anything about their backgrounds, it sure seems backwards, though. It would have been much more logical for Paul (a man thoroughly trained in rabbinical law) to be sent to the Jews. And yet, God picked another candidate: Peter. *What? Peter? That seems like a strange choice.*

Peter was a fisherman, untrained in Jewish law and, in the religious leader's eyes, a common peasant. There was no reason for them to listen to Peter or be persuaded by his argument. And yet, that was God's plan. Who else but Peter would have the audacity to stand up on the day of Pentecost and proclaim, "Let all Israel be assured of this: God has made this Jesus, whom you crucified, both Lord and Messiah"? (Acts 2:36). What an accusation!

And yet, after calling them all murderers, surprisingly, here was their response: "They were cut to the heart and said to Peter and the other apostles, 'Brothers, what shall we do?'" (Acts 2:37).

At the church's inception, God used a common peasant to execute His divine plan. His choice in Peter, not Paul, was right after all. Here's what we learn: *God's plan executed God's way always yields God's results.*

Not long after the church was founded, Peter and John were brought before the Sanhedrin and questioned. Here was the Sanhedrin's impression of the two young church leaders:

> *Now when they saw the boldness of Peter and John, and perceived that they were unlearned and ignorant men, they marveled; and they took knowledge of them, that they had been with Jesus. (Acts 4:13 KJV)*

What baffled the religious leaders were Peter and John's uncanny boldness, not their argument or knowledge of Jewish law. Although the Sanhedrin couldn't figure them out, it also couldn't disregard them. You notice God didn't use Nicodemus (one of their peers), who had met with Jesus before He was crucified and was likely in attendance.

God's destiny for our lives doesn't always look the way we think it should. Why is this? Often we look around and see what God is doing in other people's lives and assume He will (and should) do the same in ours. When we try and fail, we get frustrated, and it causes us to think to ourselves: *God, my life, family, or ministry doesn't look like that man's or woman's, so it must not be right.*

Comparison

Comparing ourselves to others can be damaging. But even more dangerous is when we try and start changing God's plan. We look at the task at hand and conclude: *This can't possibly be the right strategy.* Can you imagine Paul saying, "Hey Peter, let me handle all the Jewish debates, and why don't you take the gospel to the Gentiles."

It seems rational and a much more logical solution. Paul's credentials spoke for themselves. Side by side, Peter's knowledge and experience didn't measure up. Given the facts, it would be easy to make an adjustment.

And yet, had Paul not planted all the Gentile churches—spread out over great distances as they were—he would not have been motivated to pen the many letters of instruction. And had that not happened, we wouldn't have over a third of the New Testament.

God's plan is always best even when we don't understand it. This lack of understanding what God is actually accomplishing plays perfectly into Satan's secret of I. Fortunately, on the flipside, we find another secret in the heart of God: blind trust.

Do You Trust Me?

There was a Disney movie that came out several years ago called *Aladdin.*[4] In one particular scene, a blockade of palace guards burst through the door of Aladdin's residence to rescue the princess. The princess, however, had run away and had no desire to be rescued. Aladdin jumps to his feet and extends his hand back to her. "Do you trust me?" he exclaims. Gingerly, she nods her head yes.

A moment later Aladdin grabs her hand, and they jump through an escape hatch in the floor. While falling several stories, Aladdin creates a parachute out of cloth he grabs along the way, allowing them to land safely on the ground and escape. Hooray for the hero!

Just as Aladdin had to settle one important issue before he was able to intervene in the princess's affair, we must answer the same question from God: "Do you trust Me?" Answering this question beckons knowing one crucial thing: Is He trustworthy? I know it's easy to say He is. Yet sometimes, when our circumstances don't add up or make sense to us, it requires the secret of blind trust to answer an undeniable, unmistakable, "Yes!"

Shattered Expectations

After four years planting Worship Central Church in north San Diego, we ran about a hundred people in our fellowship. It had been a long, hard fight to gain momentum. Entering the upcoming year, I felt we finally had it.

In prayer one day, God took me to the passage in Luke where Peter and the disciples had been fishing all night without a catch (see Luke 5:4-6). Jesus shows up and asks Peter to cast his net to the other side of the boat. Solely out of obedience, Peter half-heartedly complies. To his surprise, a massive school of fish filled the net. It was a miracle!

As I read the passage, I felt the Holy Spirit whisper to me: "This is the year—the year of your miraculous catch."

I was thrilled, and since Easter was approaching, I developed a sermon series about casting the net and believing God for a harvest. Over the next few months of strategic planning, we geared up and launched a marketing campaign involving several outreaches escalating up to Easter Sunday.

During the series, however, something quite disheartening started to happen. A family met with us and informed us they were leaving the church. We were bummed, but we blessed them and tried to shake it off. Not long after, two families moved away because of sudden job transfers, and another family moved because of military deployment. Lastly, a very stable couple in the church met with us. They were having relationship problems and told us, "We are leaving to find a church with a strong counseling ministry."

In all, during those few months, six families left the church. I finished the series, and we had a wonderful Easter service with good attendance, but it was nothing like I anticipated. I was discouraged.

As the dust settled, I evaluated the outcome and realized (over about a four-month period) we had not grown miraculously but diminished dramatically.

When Peter had cast the net to the other side, the catch he received was overwhelming—even broke the net—because it was so large. I was confused. Going into summer of that same year, the church was only running about sixty people. I remember scratching my head and asking God, "What did we do wrong?"

I kept praying and seeking God but didn't seem to be getting any answers. Instead, I felt change was coming. And deep down, I also felt we were to hold steady because, somehow, we were on the right track.

Above all, I felt God asking me: "Do you trust Me?"

Church Merger

At the end of summer, I received a phone call from a local pastor in our city. We'd built a friendship over the last four years, and he'd called to see how I was doing. I didn't tell him the details but shared that I was discouraged. He offered some encouraging words and prayed with me. After the prayer, he asked me, "Would you ever consider a church merger?"

I admit I was taken back at first and replied, "Well, no. Not really."

He went on to tell me that, if I was open to it, he'd be willing to talk it over. There was no pressure, of course, but he wanted to put it out there.

I remember hanging up the phone and thinking to myself: *That'll never happen. God didn't call us halfway across the country with a vision to plant a church only to hand it over to someone else.* Yet, in the months ahead, his words almost haunted me. And at the same time, as I prayed I kept hearing God's voice asking, "Do you trust Me?"

I wrestled with it for months, and by December I could no longer ignore what I knew deep down in my heart. I called him up and said, "You mentioned a church merger. I'd like to know what your thoughts are about it and what it would look like exactly?"

After the holidays were over, we sat down to discuss it. I had done some fasting, a lot of praying, and had a good idea that God was leading us to merge. With that said, I also wanted to hear his strategy. As we talked, there was confirmation after confirmation, and by the time we laid out a plan, I knew it was go!

Miraculous Catch

Although I knew God was leading us to merge, there was one big problem: I had to convince our people this was God's doing. I called our leadership together, and, I'll say it as kindly as I can, they were not happy about it—at all. People were also very vocal about their opinion, saying, "But what about the vision God gave you? What does this mean for *our* church's identity?" Mostly, I think they picked up on what I was feeling: *We tried, and we failed.*

Over the next few weeks, I did my due diligence to meet with almost every family in our church. I tried to be as honest and transparent as possible and told them, "As much as I don't fully understand it, I feel God is in this merger." It was dicey for a while, but as I shared my heart, people started to come around to the idea.

Finally, I felt the time had come to ask the pastor to speak with our people and share his plan for the merger. More than that, I felt they needed to hear his heart as well as his vision. Going into the meeting, I was pretty nervous.

Our people crammed into our home. We did some worship, and then I turned the floor over to Pastor Aaron. For an hour, he shared his story as well as answered their questions. I watched and held my breath. It was going well. But, I also knew our people. We'd done life together, and I could see the apprehension on their faces.

Oh, God, I prayed to myself. *I know You're in this, and I trust You. Please show Yourself and bring comfort to our people. Help them see what You're doing here.*

Something shifted almost instantly. Pastor Aaron stopped and said, "I know this isn't easy. For many of you," he paused and turned to me, "including Pastor Brian, this feels like the death of a dream."

I watched closely and could tell he'd just struck a nerve; our people were listening closely and attentively. I felt it was a pivotal moment. What he said next not only shocked me but the entire group. "You know, I was on my way over here, and for some reason, I kept thinking about the passage in Luke where Jesus asked Peter to cast his net to the other side."

I gulped, stunned.

"Let me tell you what happened last year at our church. We were running about four hundred before Easter," he said, "and by the time Christmas rolled around, we were averaging over eight hundred in attendance. We over doubled in a very short amount of time. It was a total miracle, just like when Jesus asked Peter to cast the net and a miraculous catch filled those nets."

My jaw fell open and so did the rest of our people's. I was shocked and couldn't believe what I was hearing, but what came out of his mouth next blew my mind.

"On my way over here, I kept thinking about that story. If you've read it, you'll remember that Peter had to call over another boat to help bring in the harvest of fish because it was too much for him and the net was breaking. That's a spiritual snapshot of what I see God doing here. I look around this room and see leaders. I see people who really understand how to do the work of the ministry. With all the new growth, I feel God is bringing laborers to help us gather in this miraculous catch."

As I glanced around the room, I knew God had just answered my prayer. The looks of apprehension were gone!

I also realized, along with me, the people wondered why God hadn't brought the growth we'd anticipated last year. Little did we know that, from Easter to Christmas of that same year, a church ten minutes away from us was reaping the harvest. And little did we know that God would partner us together to help gather the miraculous catch.

Through the experience, I learned firsthand that doing things God's way brings God-sized results—even when we don't understand or see what God is doing.

Leading up to the church merger, how many times did my pride tell me, "You're wrong. You missed it. Why give your flock over to someone else's vision?" All the while God was asking: "Do you trust Me?"

I'm not sure if Peter ever wondered: *Why am I the one preaching to the Jews?* I'm not sure if Paul wondered the same about preaching to the Gentiles. *What I am sure of is this: God has more than proven His plan is best—even when I don't understand.* As much as Satan tries to convince us otherwise, the secret of blind trust helps us confidently proclaim, "God, I trust You because You are trustworthy!"

CHAPTER 4

Secret of Others

ALTHOUGH THERE IS a countless number of books written on the subject of wisdom, there is none more important or profound than the book of Proverbs. In it, Solomon teaches us, "The beginning of wisdom is this: Get wisdom. Though it cost all you have" (Prov 4:7). Sounds simple right? Just get wisdom—even if it makes you bankrupt. *Hmm? Maybe not so easy after all.*

As true and significant as this request is, perhaps like many, you've found it difficult to achieve. There is a quote by Otto von Bismarck, German Chancellor between 1862 and 1890, that seems to epitomize how we can achieve it:

"A fool learns from his mistakes, but a truly wise man learns from the mistakes of others."[5]

When it comes to gaining wisdom from the mistakes of others, there's no better place to glean from than Scripture. The Bible is full of examples of men and women who fell prey to Satan's secret of I. Learning from their mistakes saves us from falling into the same disastrous traps.

Samson

When I was a child, I heard stories about Samson, the strongest man who ever lived. The picture of Samson I've painted in my mind would be comparable to a superhero with muscles popping out everywhere and displaying great feats of strength unaccomplished by any other human man. Yet, there was another side, often overlooked, that demonstrated weakness of character and frailty of human spirit. Although ordained by God to wreak havoc on his Philistine neighbors, his life was plagued with moral defeats.

The first sign we have of Samson's lack of character comes in his request for the hand of a Philistine girl from the neighboring village of Timnah. Actually, *request* would be much too timid a word; Samson *demanded* the arrangement. His parents pleaded with him to marry one of the daughters from the tribes of Israel, but he would not listen. He was determined to have her, saying "Get her for me; for she pleases me well" (Judg 14:3b).

Apparently, Samson had already slept with the girl, and being satisfied, he demanded to make her his wife. This was just one of three accounts in which he was involved in an inappropriate relationship, two of which, more than likely, involved prostitutes.

Surely, his parents must have told him about his miraculous birth. You would think they must have told him about their encounter with the messenger of God. Before Samson was even born, the angel told them, "The boy is to be a Nazirite, set apart for God from birth and he will begin the deliverance of Israel from the hand of the Philistines" (Judg 13:5).

There's no doubt Samson was chosen for a divine purpose. Unfortunately, Satan's secret of I had infiltrated Samson's thinking. As we'll discover, the exploits fulfilling God's destiny—bringing havoc to the Philistines—was done, many times, for selfish reasons. On one such occasion, Samson says, "This time I have a right to get even with the Philistines" (Judg 15:3). Later he explains, "Since you've acted like this, I won't stop until I get my revenge on you [the Philistines]" (Judg 15:7).

To get a better understanding, let's look at Samson's accomplishments:

FEATS OF STRENGTH	REASON FOR ACTION
Killed a lion with his bare hands.	*It was an act of self-defense.*
Killed thirty Philistines.	*Losing a bet, he killed them to acquire payment.*
Caught three hundred foxes.	*A torch was tied to every pair, and then they were released into the Philistine villages because his wife was given to his best man.*
Killed a thousand Philistines.	*With the jawbone of a donkey, he retaliated after they burned his wife alive.*
Carried the city gates of Gaza.	*Leaving a prostitute's house, he tore them off the hinges and toted them to a nearby hilltop for no apparent reason.*
Destroyed the temple of Dagon.	*Pushing the pillars off their foundation, the temple crashed down on the Philistine leaders (Samson was slain also that day).*

These are the major accomplishments in Samson's life. You be the judge. Do you think this is all God had ordained him to do?

As I see it, there were only three events bringing any kind of significant damage to the Philistines. In the rest, Samson displayed tremendous strength, but the events themselves had no real purpose in fulfilling God's destiny for his life.

Even at the highlight of Samson's life—the moment when everyone thought he had finally learned his lesson—his character flaws shine through. After convincing a servant boy to let him place his hands on the pillars, he prays this pathetic prayer: "Oh Sovereign Lord, remember me. O God, please strengthen me just once more, and let me with one blow get revenge on the Philistines for my two eyes" (Judg 16:28).

Poor Samson just didn't get it. It was all about him, wasn't it? Every blow inflicted to the Philistines was a retaliation of something they'd done to him. Here was someone with supernatural strength ordained to do more damage to the Philistines as a single man than the entire tribes of Israel combined. Yet, due to pride and selfish motives, he was forced to entertain the crowd with eyes gouged out between two pillars. God was gracious, however, and gave him back his strength and used his triumphant death as a victory for Israel despite his selfish thinking.

Perhaps this was the only way God could get through Samson's stubbornness to fulfill his destiny. Had he stayed away from Delilah and other women, following after God wholeheartedly, he could have simply showed up at the same Philistine temple, walked through the front door, and destroyed just as many.

In his *Layman's Bible Book Commentary*, Dan G. Kent states,

> *"This is not a very uplifting story. Samson was a weakling in every way that counted. The record of his profligate life is reported more for warning than for example."*[6]

The Elders of Israel

Israel was in a time of disorganization. They had judges in the past (such as Samson), but somehow this seemed inadequate. The elders of Israel went to Samuel to cry out for a leader: a king who would rule, reign, and lead them into battle. Samuel was displeased. For in doing so, God made it clear: "They have rejected Me as their king" (1 Sam 8:7).

In retrospect, it was a terrible mistake. Even after being warned of the consequences, Israel would not listen. They said, "No! We want a king over us. Then we will be like other nations, with a king to lead us and to go out before us and fight our battles" (1 Sam 8:19).

Why did Israel want a king? Think about it. They looked around at other nations and thought: *Hey wait a minute. Everyone has a king except us. We're not like everyone else, so something must be wrong.*

Here's the truth of the matter: Israel was never meant to be like the other nations of the world. They were chosen—set apart, just as we are a chosen people and royal priesthood (see 1 Pet 2:9).

Israel's decision resulted in a curse: "When the day comes you will cry out for relief from the king you have chosen, and the Lord will not answer you in that day" (1 Sam 8:18). Even more deadly than Satan's secret of I in an individual is pride in a corporate assembly. Not only were the elders putting their own livelihood on the line, but that of their children and generations to come.

King Nebuchadnezzar

In the book of Daniel, we see another account of Satan's secret of I at work. While standing on the roof of the royal palace of Babylon, King Nebuchadnezzar made this statement: "Is not this a great Babylon I have built as the royal residence, by my mighty power and for the glory of my majesty?" (Dan 4:30).

What a claim. Though it's something many men may have thought about themselves, it's something very few would have the audacity to make. *Aren't I great? Look at what I've done.*

It's important to note where power and authority truly come from: "For there is no power but from God; the powers that be are ordained by God" (Rom 13:1). We further learn this when Jesus stood before Pilate and informed him, "You would have no power over me if it were not given to you from above" (John 19:11). Jesus submitted himself to Pilate understanding who was really in charge. Ultimately, it wasn't Pilate he was submitting himself to, but it was to God.

In turn, we could also conclude*: Anything we accomplish or achieve in this lifetime is the direct result of God's power and authority at work in and through us.* Unfortunately, King Nebuchadnezzar didn't discover this secret until too late.

Let's look at God's response:

> *The words were still on his lips when a voice came from heaven, "This is what is decreed for you, King*

Nebuchadnezzar: Your royal authority has been taken from you. You will be driven away from people and will live with the wild animals; you will eat grass like cattle. Seven times will pass by for you until you acknowledge that the Most High is sovereign over the kingdoms of men and gives them to anyone he wishes." (Dan 4:31-32)

In judgment, God responded from heaven saying, "So, king, you think you're hot stuff. Since you are acting like an animal, I'll treat you like one until you repent and acknowledge Me as Lord of the universe!"

God Doesn't Need Me

I remember getting up to lead worship one Sunday morning. I had my song list made out as usual and stepped behind the keyboard. Any worship leader can relate to this. Sometimes, you get up and every song seems to take off. Other times, everything goes over like a lead balloon.

On this particular service—from the get-go—people began to enter in and worship with all their hearts. It seemed every song I'd selected was a winner and perfect for the moment.

Before long, we were in the very throne room of God. People were bowing on their knees, hands were raised, and tears were flowing. I stopped playing and backed away from the keyboard, and people began to lift their voices in spontaneous worship across the congregation. Lifting my hands and closing my eyes, I joined in as well. It was a marvelous move of the Holy Spirit.

After a few minutes, I opened my eyes to look out across the sanctuary, and this thought came to my mind:

You did a great job today. If it weren't for you, these people wouldn't be in the presence of God right now. They sure are lucky to have you.

I was shocked! *Where in the world did that come from?* I immediately discarded the thought and continued worshiping.

You might be wondering: *Whoa, Brian! That sounds so horrible—how could you even think such a thought like that?*

The sad truth is, it's human nature, as King Nebuchadnezzar did, to take ownership of something that is not ours. Just as the king stood gazing over his kingdom, I stood that day looking over my area of influence, and those fleshly, animal-like instincts welled up inside me.

We all have this tendency. It is a part of our nature. Although we can't help the initial thought, our job is to take that thought captive and bring it to the obedience of Christ (see 1 Cor 10:5). King Nebuchadnezzar, however, embraced these thoughts of pride and even went on to speak them out. And he paid dearly.

The Temptation of Success

Moses stretched his rod over the Red Sea, and before the eyes of millions of Israelites, the water parted in two. While in his teens, David stepped up defeating Goliath in front of all the warriors of Israel. Can you imagine if you or I were Moses or David at that moment? Do you know how easy it would have been to ingest the moment, thinking, *Wow, look what I did! I saved the whole nation!*

During my son's teenage years, I was adamant about teaching him to memorize Scripture. Each day on the way to school we'd quote handpicked verses I felt crucial for his spiritual development. This verse was the very first one I taught him: "No temptation has seized you except what is common to man, and God is faithful, he will not let you be tempted beyond what you can bear" (1 Cor 10:13). The reason I chose this verse first is because of something I heard my father pray over me and my brothers while we were growing up, "Let my boys be strong in adversity and humble in success."

I am very encouraged by the fact every temptation I face won't go beyond my capacity to bear it. And yet, there's something in my dad's request I can't get away from: "humble in success." Thinking about that verse, have you ever considered that success could be a temptation?

Many cry out for God to use them mightily and then wonder why it doesn't happen (at least to their level of expectation). God is smarter than that. Think about what might have happened if it were you or I who walked in David's shoes? I'm almost positive I couldn't have killed a nine-foot giant with a sling. Why? Because I probably would have let it go to my head.

Before I throw David under the bus here, know that I'm his biggest fan—even wrote books on his life. And yet, if you look at his motives in fighting Goliath, I find they were mixed. The young shepherd boy who had been anointed by Samuel as the next king of Israel saw an opportunity. After seeing Goliath, he not only asked, "Who is this uncircumcised Philistine," but, "What will be done for the man who kills him?" (see 1 Sam 17:26).

After David's triumph over Goliath (leading to his stardom), it's worth noting that much rejection followed. I wonder if, in the years following such a momentous victory, that's exactly what David needed. I wonder if this was God's "way of escape" from the temptation of success.

I find there are two forms of temptation—two approaches—Satan uses to trip us up: rejection and praise. Both can be equally destructive. It's like a two-edged sword. Both are sharp, and both will cut you, just from different angles. If the enemy can't bring you down with failure, sometimes he will try and build up your successes and tempt your ego. I've found those pats on the back, high fives, and kind words of "great job" are only as important as you make them.

The Power of Repentance

Although Samson, the elders of Israel, and King Nebuchadnezzar are examples of people who crashed and burned, there are many who didn't. While from these three examples we learn what not to do, there are remarkable examples of those who accomplished much and served well without faltering. Individuals like Samuel, Enoch, Joseph, and Job all left fine examples for us to follow.

Even more fascinating are those who had huge blunders and, after learning their lessons, repented, overcame, and went on to do great exploits. Surprisingly, years later, after becoming king, David is a great example of this. I find hope for my own journey in studying and gleaning from David's life, both his successes and his failures.

First, I want to point out David was called *a man after God's own heart.* In a book such as this—about discovering the secret heart of God—how intriguing a statement. Is that even possible? Can a man have the same heart as God? Because of the secret of others, we learn David actually epitomized, and was known as, a man after God's own heart. Fascinating!

The more I study his life, the more I believe what made David a man after God's own heart was not his ability to refrain from sinning, but rather his elaborate and headlong way of repenting. After being called on the carpet by Nathan the prophet for committing adultery and murder, his child (from the affair) died at the hand of God's judgment. And what was David's response? After cleaning himself up, he went into the house of God and worshiped.

I have no evidence David wrote the following Psalm during that worship time, but we do know, at a minimum, it was written in response to his affair:

> *Have mercy on me, O God, according to your unfailing love; according to your great compassion blot out my transgressions. Wash away all my iniquity and cleanse me from my sin. For I know my transgressions, and my sin is always before me. Against you, you only, have I sinned. (Ps 51:1-4a)*

The verses following David's prayer of repentance take an awkward turn. In fact, like David tended to do, he invented terminology never before expressed in worship. When David cried out using such extreme vernacular as, "deliver me...or they will tear me apart like a lion and rip me to pieces" (Ps 7:1b-2), or, "I am a worm and not a man, scorned by everyone" (Ps 22:6), I wonder what people thought? People probably scratched their heads and thought: *What did David just say? What in the world is he talking about?*

I don't believe God did. God knew exactly what David meant. In fact, the Almighty seemed to love David's raw candor and vulnerability—even at a time like this. After taking full responsibility for his actions, with a heart of repentance, David cries: “Cleanse me with hyssop, and I will be clean; wash me, and I will be whiter than snow” (Ps 51:7).

Hyssop? Really David—why hyssop?

First off, there were only a few uses for hyssop in the Old Testament. In Leviticus, we learn priests used hyssop, a minty plant, in a ceremony to pronounce a formerly diseased person as clean (see Lev 14:1-7). The same method was used to purify a house that had previously contained mold (see Lev 14:33-53). Lastly, when the Israelites marked their doorposts with lamb’s blood in order for the angel of death to pass over them, God instructed them to use hyssop as a paintbrush (Exod 12:22).

So, what was David’s deal here? Why speak of hyssop in one of his most turbulent times. He’d sinned greatly and everyone knew about it. And in that disenchanted moment, why would David cry out, “Cleanse me with hyssop?”

During his most grueling moments on the cross, a Roman guard took a sponge filled with bitter wine, placed it on, of all things, a hyssop branch and lifted it up to Jesus’ lips. This was, in fact, Jesus’ last act before He declared His work on earth finished and gave up His spirit. How interesting that David, a type of Christ and man after God’s own heart, cried out, “Cleanse me with hyssop,” during his moment of despair.

Just before Jesus encountered the bitter drink, He had cried out, “I am thirsty?” What was he thirsty for? I believe it’s the same thing David was thirsty for. Not wine. Not water or drink of any kind. It was for forgiveness! It was for healing, cleansing, and relief from the agony of his sin. It was the same thing Jesus, who carried our sin, was thirsty for. In a moment chillingly paralleled with His

Son on the cross, God heard David's cry for repentance and forgave him.

I imagine God, who doesn't operate in time and space as we do, listening to David's cry for hyssop and thinking: *Hmm? Where have I seen hyssop before?* Looking over at Jesus, already slain for mankind, he relishes: *Oh yes, Son, I remember now.*

David certainly knew how to get God's attention. We can learn a great deal from him, even from the times when he blew it badly. Although he had some huge blunders, he was still called *a man after God's own heart.* Why? Because David repented well.

I'm No David

The secret of learning from others, such as King David, can be powerful and life changing, but I wonder if you're thinking: *That's great, but I'm no David.*

Yes, it's true. David was the only person in Scripture called *a man after God's own heart.* But, surprisingly, you don't have to be one of Israel's greatest worshipers or a brave shepherd boy who fought and defeated a giant to repent well.

Let's learn from a very unlikely character we've already discussed: King Nebuchadnezzar. When we left him, he was eating grass and living as an animal out in the open field. Yikes! Then something changed—he looked up!

> *At the end of that time, I, Nebuchadnezzar, raised my eyes toward heaven, and my sanity was restored. At the same time that my sanity was restored, my honor and splendor were returned to me for the glory of my kingdom. My advisers and nobles sought me out, and I was restored to my*

> *throne and became even greater than before. Now I, Nebuchadnezzar, praise and exalt and glorify the King of heaven, because everything he does is right and all his ways are just. And those who walk in pride he is able to humble. (Dan 4:34a, 36-37)*

Using the secret of others, what can we learn from the humbled king? Repentance works. Remarkably, not just for King David, but for King Nebuchadnezzar. When I reflect on this verse, another reassuring thought comes to mind: *If God can do it for a wicked and prideful Babylonian king, he can do it for me—and you.*

In her article, "Nobody's Hopeless," daughter of Billy Graham, Anne Graham Lotz said it this way:

"And he [King Nebuchadnezzar] is the ruler Saddam Hussein said he wanted to be like. This same Nebuchadnezzar was converted! And he wrote down his testimony as a witness not only to the world of his day, but also to future generations."[7]

You may be saying, "I'm no David." Come here. Lean in and let me tell you a secret: God didn't only respond to David. He also responded to Nebuchadnezzar's cry of repentance.

Who knows? Perhaps the title to the article Anne wrote is right: Nobody's hopeless.

CHAPTER 5

Secret of Humility

EVERY YEAR IN SCHOOL, there was a week set aside for state testing. One section, in particular, caught my interest:

Choose the term that best describes the opposite of the word front.

a) rear

b) behind

c) back

d) reverse *Answer: c*

Choose the term that best describes the opposite of the word loud.

a) soft

b) quiet

c) silent

d) whisper *Answer: a*

Choose the term that best describes the opposite of the word proud.

a) sincere

b) timid

c) questionable

d) humble *Answer: d*

It is easier to understand what a word means when you understand its opposite. We find meaning in the word *over* by knowing what it is to go *under.* We find meaning in the word *son* by knowing the opposite is *daughter.* We can find deeper meaning in the word *pride* by understanding its opposite: *humility.* Thus, a simple definition of pride could be the opposite of humble or not humble.

If pride is the place where sin gets its root, I believe there is no greater attribute that exemplifies the secret heart of God than humility. And there is no greater example of humility than Jesus on the cross: "And being found in fashion as a man, he humbled himself, and became obedient unto death, even the death of the cross" (Phil 2:8 KJV).

I've often wondered why Satan, who, believe it or not, knows the Bible, would kill Jesus ultimately leading to his own demise and our salvation. I can't pretend to know the answer with certainty. But, I do know that Satan was the epitome of pride, and the world's stage was likely too tempting an offer for him to refuse. After taking the floor, he made full use of the most horrific execution techniques known to man.

Some translations declare Jesus was so mangled, He was beyond recognition: "But many were amazed when they saw him. His face was so disfigured he seemed hardly human, and from his appearance, one would scarcely know he was a man" (Isa 52:14 NLT).

Few realize the agony Jesus endured. Naked and beaten beyond human recognition, Jesus suffered in a way no one can imagine. While on the cross, Satan gloated over Him, mocking Him relentlessly. Meanwhile, Jesus gained for us what we could never achieve. I love the way The Living Bible translates this verse: "In this way God took away Satan's power to accuse you of sin, and God openly displayed to the whole world Christ's triumph at the cross where your sins were all taken away" (Col 2:15).

In his pride, Satan flaunted his opportunity to make a public spectacle of Jesus' suffering. Jesus, on the other hand, openly displayed His humble heart to humanity. What a beautiful glimpse into the secret heart of God and a perfect description of humility.

I'll Make Myself Go to Sleep

I was leading worship each night at a series of special services at our church. The last service of the event ended on Sunday evening. After two Sunday morning services and one evening service, I was extremely tired. Knowing what a long day I'd had, my wife let me off the hook in helping get the kids bathed, dressed, and tucked in bed.

Sometimes getting three little ones to bed is not any easy task. In the other room I heard the racket. My oldest daughter Breanne was doing her usual "I'm not tired" routine while Kaitlin and Tyler were crying due to being at church all day long.

While my wife put the kids to bed, I got ready and was lying in bed. I didn't really have peace and quiet until my wife came to bed about twenty minutes later. *Uh-oh!* Just after she slipped in bed, piercing the darkness was the cutest voice you've ever heard, "Mommy, I'm thirsty! Can I have a drink of water?" My wife turned and gave me *the look*. When she gives me that look, I know that's it! She's had it up to here, and I'd better step in. So, I did what any loving father and husband should do in this situation and yelled back, "You can wait until morning, now go to sleep!" Not a chance. After the fourth time, I mustered all my strength to get my little girl a glass of water and then scurried back to bed.

Now I don't know what happened, but at the very instant I turned off the light switch, it was like a sensor went off in my brain and my eyes popped open. For about five minutes, I laid there looking at the ceiling. Then I glanced over at the clock. Then back to the ceiling. Then back at the clock. *What's wrong with me? Why in the world am I still awake?*

Here I was absolutely exhausted, lying in a comfortable bed and not able to go to sleep. My amazement turned to concern and eventually to frustration. Then, suddenly, I had the most brilliant idea: *I know—I'll make myself go to sleep*. I've heard people say it before, "Just close your eyes and force your body to go to sleep." Being so tired, I figured it shouldn't be too hard. So, I gave it a try. I tried. And I tried. Then I tried some more until I was all tried out.

It was at this point that I heard a still small voice whisper to me, "You can't make yourself go to sleep." *That's funny. Why would God tell me something like that?* As I laid there awhile and listened more intently, my thoughts turned to this book. He spoke to me again and said, "You can't make yourself go to sleep, just like you can't make pride leave your life." Eventually, I went to sleep only after I learned the important secret God was teaching me.

Here's the lesson: *You can't make the pride disappear any more than you can make yourself go to sleep.* What you can do is create an environment that is sleep-friendly. You can create an atmosphere that promotes falling asleep: darkness, silence (or constant noise), a warm cozy bed, lying down (at the appropriate time), and so on. The same is true with overcoming Satan's secret of I. You can create an environment that promotes the opposite: humility.

Doing the Opposite

As I've thought long and hard on the subject, I don't know of a way to set an atmosphere of humility better than servanthood. Here's my practical definition of servanthood: doing the opposite of the flesh. Servanthood is cheerfully fulfilling God-ordained tasks in which the flesh says, "No, no, no," and the Spirit says "Yes, yes, yes."

You cannot convince me Jesus' flesh felt like washing the disciples' feet on the night He was to be betrayed, accused, ridiculed, and beaten. How do I know? Because, hours later, He sweated great drops of blood and pleaded with His Father to take the cup from Him. His flesh was saying, "No, no, no!" But, His spirit was saying, "Yes, yes, yes! Not My will but Yours be done." He grabbed the basin and towel and cheerfully taught the disciples a lesson that would get them through some of the toughest times in their life of ministry. It was the lesson of servanthood.

In this passage, Jesus has set the ultimate example of humility:

> *"Whoever wishes to be great among you must be your servant. And whoever desires to be first among you must be your slave, just as the Son of man came not to be waited on but to serve, and to give His life as a ransom for many." (Matt 20:27-28 AMP)*

Christ-like service is at the center of the heart of God. But be forewarned, this caliber of humility comes at great cost. It is the epitome of a laid-down life on behalf of others. For many people, it's a price too high to pay!

Let me give you some practical suggestions on service that promotes humility:

1. Volunteer for a task you think you are too good for.
2. Spend the day with someone who drives you crazy.
3. Volunteer to clean your church's toilets for a day.

These three jobs (put together) parallel Jesus' example of service when He washed His disciples' feet in Luke 22. As their leader and supposed Messiah, He should have been the last to wash feet. If anything, they should have washed His feet. Thus, He fulfilled task number one.

With the hodge-podge group of misfits He had assembled, I'm sure the disciples were very annoying at times—particularly Peter. There's number two.

The sanitation system of the ancient world was non-existent. Since the sandal was the common shoe of the day, Jesus might as well have been cleaning toilets—not just human, but animal toilets. Number three down.

Jesus used an object lesson that night of choosing acts of service. By doing the opposite of His flesh, Jesus set an atmosphere of humility. Hours later, in the garden, it was almost as if, when tempted by Satan's secret of I, Jesus confidently replied, "I already chose to serve at the Last Supper, and, in turn, I'll gladly take the cup the Father has prepared for me."

A Marriage Saved

A friend told me about a time when his marriage was failing. His actions through the years had brought much anguish to his wife—causing deep wounds to form in their relationship. As he was telling the story he made this statement, "I hope you never know how it feels to say 'I love you' to your wife only to get a blank stare in return." He went on, "I wasn't sure she loved me anymore—but I had to try to salvage our marriage."

Both individuals were very godly people. He tried to mend the relationship every way he knew how, but it just wasn't working. So he began to pray. Finally, there was a glimmer of hope. One day while in prayer, God spoke to his wife saying, "Each day you need to do one nice thing for this man, or you'll never love him again."

It was difficult for her at first, but she fulfilled God's request. Every day she made a conscious decision to perform a good deed for her husband. It started small like making him a cup of coffee or giving him a glass of water and grew into something bigger like packing his lunch or ironing his clothes. Eventually, her feelings began to return, but it was only after she humbled herself by serving him. Today, this couples' marriage is strong and vibrant, and they are helping other men and women who have lost all hope for their marriages.

What I find fascinating about this story is how the marriage was saved. You notice it wasn't marriage counseling. Neither was it a sermon or marriage retreat—all of which I'm very much in favor of. This godly woman prayed and found the answer to save her marriage: It was servanthood.

I'm sure many times this godly wife thought of giving up: *Why do I need to do anything for him? He hurt me!* If she had given in to what her flesh was saying, I'm quite sure her marriage would have ended in divorce. Despite her sinful nature, she was humble enough to do it God's way, accepting the fact it wouldn't be easy.

Humility in Servanthood

Through the years, I've had the privilege of mentoring a host of worship leaders, singers, musicians, and ministry leaders. One such opportunity was at Christ for the Nations Institute in Dallas, where we attracted students with amazing talent from all over the world. To all the new worship students each semester, I made it a point to share, "It's unfortunate that many of you with the most talent will be used the least."

I'd always get blank stares. And yet, as the year unfolded, I found it to be true. I saw many of the most talented students who didn't take on an attitude of servanthood quickly fall to the wayside. Some would get suspended due to character issues. Many were unwilling to submit to the process or structure of worship we'd established and were demoted. I could always tell those who were solely seeking the spotlight by their attitude of servanthood—or lack thereof.

As I've discovered, if you desire to be used by God and have ever prayed for the opportunity, God will test you. Without fail, a week or a month down the road an opportunity would present itself: "Hey Brian, they need some volunteers down at the senior center to play games with the old folks," or, "They're serving food down at the homeless shelter and need help." I learned quickly the desire to be used by God meant one thing—serving!

In worship ministry, I always needed people to help set up or tear down equipment, or come early to help with worship preparation. As I rose in leadership, I always looked for those with a servant's heart willing to do what others weren't. And many times, those students were the same ones I promoted to significant roles in ministry.

God Knows Your Desires

I was asked to lead worship at a fun, lighthearted Marriage and Family Seminar on the coast. I accepted the invitation and was excited about the opportunity, as well as getting to spend a few days at the beach.

The services were powerful. On Saturday morning, the speaker talked about anger in the home, and after a call was given, the altars were filled. I was on stage singing softly and saw hundreds of husbands and wives turning to each other asking for forgiveness. I was deeply touched and even remember crying, which made it hard to sing.

Although the final service on Sunday morning was life-changing, it also went very long—much longer than I anticipated. Now I failed to mention that, when I accepted the invitation, I also assured my pastor we would be back in time for a Sunday evening event. This meant we had to pack up all our instruments, eat a bite, drive two-and-a-half hours, and set up everything again in one afternoon. Since the service went long that morning, our timetable was tight, and we were running late.

Even worse than being late, I found out just before service we had a last-minute guest speaker. We were tired. We were frazzled and without much of a sound-check, our monitor mixes were sub-par. It was so bad, in fact, we had feedback problems that caused the monitors to squeal during the first song.

Before starting the second song, I said, "As you can tell we're having some sound issues. Let's just try to look past all that's going wrong and do our best to worship God." This helped a little, but I still didn't feel good about the worship time. After worship, I hung my head and stammered off the stage glad it was finally over.

I went back to get some water and then slipped quietly back into the sanctuary to find my seat. They had already introduced the speaker by this time. I had no idea who he was or where he came from. As I was getting ready to sit down, he said, "Where's the worship leader?" I've never wanted to hide so badly in all my life, but I sheepishly raised my hand and came forward. As soon as I reached the stage he said, "God told me to tell you that it's time you make a worship album."

You've got to be kidding me? Didn't you see what a mess I made out of that worship set?

He went on, "God says you have a heart that is pure. It is a heart like that of David, a man after God's own heart."

Is he really talking to me? No, no mister, I thought. *God has showed me how prideful I am and how wrong my motives are. You've got the wrong guy.*

Then he said something I'll never forget, "Since you've humbled yourself and set your heart on pleasing God, He's giving you the desires of your heart. Yes, you are going to make not one, but many worship albums—not for you but for God."

After he was done, I went back to my seat and sat there utterly amazed. How could he have known? I didn't know him. He'd never seen me before that day. But God did. In fact, God knew months earlier, at a worship conference, I kneeled at the altar and prayed: *God, I want to please You. I want what You want and not what I want for my life. Lord I lay down my foolish ambitions of fame—to make a name for myself with the talent You gave me.* And this was the hard part: *God I don't care if I ever make a worship album because I just want to please You.* I said it honestly and with my entire being. And after I prayed it, I walked away thinking: *That's it—it will never happen.*

As I sat in my seat, pondering his words, Psalms 37:4 kept running across my mind: "Delight yourself in the Lord and He will give you the desires of your heart." Since that time, God has fulfilled many of my dreams. I've written and recorded songs that have been used for worship all over the world.

Here's the truth and the secret I discovered that has changed my life: Since I'd truly laid down my selfish desires in my heart, it didn't mean as much to me as it used to. I was honestly okay walking through life without ever recording or having musical success. If God allowed me to, that was fine. If God didn't, that was fine too. Like Jesus at the Last Supper, I'd already made my decision in advance to take whatever cup the Father had prepared.

God-Ordained Fast

Following the service, I felt led by the Holy Spirit to fast until God confirmed His word. Some people tell me how glorious they feel when fasting. I'll tell you how I feel most of the time—extremely hungry! This was the first extended fast I'd ever done, so I was quite consumed by it. I wasn't sure how long it was going to last and, quite frankly, that was the thing that scared me.

Ten days later, I walked into our Wednesday morning prayer meeting completely innocent as to what was going on when I arrived. Come to find out, an intercessor from another church had come over to minister. I went in and quietly sat down on the back seat. It wasn't thirty seconds before she dropped what she was doing, walked straight back towards me, laid her hand on my head, and said, "There's been something you've wanted to do for a long time. God says go ahead and do it because He's with you."

Over the course of the next several months, I saw miracle after miracle. I also began writing music at an astounding rate. Not only did God start giving me songs and ideas for the album, but a few months later, someone handed me an envelope saying, "God spoke to me to give you this." I opened it up and, surprisingly, found ten thousand dollars inside!

Here's what I've learned about humility. *When we humble ourselves and place our dreams in the hands of God, what's impossible suddenly becomes possible.* It's as if God takes our dreams and says: "These are just okay...I can do better!" When He makes the adjustments and hands them back to us, they're suddenly bigger than we'd ever imagined. And here's the good news. He not only anoints and equips us with His power to accomplish those dreams, He also promises to pay for it all. From the time I first recorded and now seven albums later—I've never lacked for the money or resources. Why? Since it was God's idea, He will make sure you have all the resources needed.

The Cost of Humility

A rich young man approached Jesus one day asking, "What must I do to inherit eternal life?" (Matt 19:16) Jesus gave him the spiel about keeping the commandments, which he had supposedly done faithfully since his youth. Then, to the amazement of all those listening, Jesus responded, "If you want to be perfect, go, sell your possessions and give them to the poor, and you will have treasures in heaven. Then come, follow me" (Matt 19:21).

The rich young ruler was in search of something. No doubt, he had already consulted the religious leaders about the same issue. I'm curious what their response was? I'm sure they commended the young man's good works. Yet, although he had great wealth and great religious traditions, he was still longing for something greater. Surprisingly, he still wasn't sure about his salvation. Unfortunately, Jesus' price for that assurance was too hard a bargain for the young man, and Scripture states, "He went away sad, because he had great wealth" (Matt 19:22).

Humility will cost you everything. There was hope for the rich young ruler, just as there is hope for you and me. The real question is whether we want to pay the price. The cost of humility is a do or die, no retreat—no surrender—kind of decision.

Who's to say this man wouldn't have been selected as one of the twelve disciples. He probably had ability running out his ears. God needs a good businessman. He needs skilled musicians. He needs good orators. He needs good doctors, good lawyers, good college professors, and other professionals. Yet I find, the majority of the time, those with great skills in their profession have a hard time humbling themselves enough to be used by God. Instead, they are looking for a list of dos and don'ts—a spiritual checklist—not truly surrendering everything to God.

It's amazing how Jesus looked right past the rich man's checklist and pointed out the elephant in the room: "You love money too much!" In one statement, Jesus identified the root problem—his pride and reluctance to trust God instead of his wealth. To everyone's surprise, Jesus went a step further and tells him the cost: everything!

You may be thinking: *That seems like too high a price. How could God require so much—everything! Really?* And here lies the problem why many receive little from the Lord. They want to come to God on their terms, not realizing that God has come to them on His terms. Is there anything more God could give to humanity than offering His only Son Jesus? Absolutely not! God offered His most precious possession, Jesus, who willingly and humbly chose to sacrifice His life on Calvary's cross.

I find, like the rich young ruler, many want to accept Jesus as their Savior, but refuse to make Jesus their Lord. It is impossible for Jesus to be your Savior without making Him your Lord. Lordship is the control issue many are unwilling to give up. Why? It's too high a price!

To a man seeking to follow Him, Jesus replied, "Foxes have holes and birds of the air have nests, but the Son of Man has no place to lay his head" (Luke 9:58). Another man approached Jesus to follow but first had to go bury his father. Jesus replied, "Let the dead bury their own dead, but you go proclaim the kingdom of God" (Luke 9:60). Still another had to go back and say goodbye to his family. Jesus replied, "No one who puts his hand to the plow and looks back is fit for service in the kingdom of God" (Luke 9:62).

What was the secret Jesus communicated in each of these examples? Humility will cost you everything! Humility for the rich young man required giving up his wealth—something that was very precious to him.

In searching for the secret of God's heart, what will humility require of you? All that is precious. Perhaps even your life. And yet, giving up our lives, our identities, and our control of our destinies lead to life everlasting. As each of the disciples found out, every sacrifice was worth it. Unlike the rich young ruler, this ragtag group of unknown fishermen, accountants, and trade professionals changed the world!

CHAPTER 6

Secret of Waiting

I BOUGHT A NICE NEW computer a few years ago. The dealer assured me it would last a long time. Come to find out, just five years later the computer is outdated. It's not that it doesn't work, but it can't keep up with the rate things are moving any longer. We live in a world that is rapidly speeding up every day. Does this sound familiar?

While out watering the lawn, I saw my next-door neighbors pull up their minivan into their driveway. Three seconds later, the garage door opened, and they pulled inside. The garage door closed, and they were gone—for the rest of the night. No contact, no hassles, and no worries.

Today, everything is based on convenience. Have you noticed that practically everything can be done from your car now? We have drive-thru banks, drive-thru pharmacies, drive-thru cleaners, drive-thru coffee places, drive-thru weddings in Las Vegas, and the list goes on and on. There's a fast food restaurant practically on every corner. I've even heard of a church somewhere that has drive-thru church services. Is this trend toward convenience wrong?

I'm not sure how I feel about drive-thru church services, but I wouldn't say convenience is necessarily bad. With that said, however, we must understand God is not a God of convenience. Let's face the facts: Anything worthwhile you accomplish for God may not be easy. Let me phrase it another way: *Many significant things God asks of us will be difficult, uncomfortable, and inconvenient.*

God's Calendar

It's easy to read the Bible without taking into consideration the time lapses that occur between different events. Some people in the Bible are only noted for one or two events that mark a change in an entire nation. There were whole life spans of waiting before God's promises were fulfilled. There were seasons of hope, and there were seasons of despair. Beyond doubt, the majority of their lives were spent pouring out all the passion they possessed into fulfilling God's task. Their blood, sweat, and tears showed God how serious they were about His promises.

With that in mind, think about this Scripture for a minute: "But, beloved, do not forget this one thing, that with the Lord one day is as a thousand years, and a thousand years as one day" (2 Pet 3:8 NKJV).

Do you realize what this verse means? This may answer a lot of questions for you: God is on a different time schedule than we are. We cry out for a week, a month, or even a year, asking God to move. When it doesn't happen right away, we give up. God's looking down from heaven thinking, *Good grief, you cried out for .007 seconds, and you expect Me to bring all of this to pass.* Sometimes we need to lay our conveniences aside, realizing what we're waiting for is not going to happen right away and allow God to work in His time.

Oh, but we don't like to wait. When the drive thru at McDonald's is taking too long, we start coming unglued. I'm sorry, but I don't care how much you honk your horn and complain; you're at the mercy of McDonald's. Complaining tends to be like running through a pool of water. The more you complain, the deeper the water gets and the slower you go. The resistance of the water greatly retards the speed at which complainers can move. Why? Because *complaining is telling God, "You don't know what You're doing!"*

If I Were God

Years ago, I saw the animated movie *Prince of Egypt*. This movie depicts the life of Moses from his birth all the way to the amazing miracle at the Red Sea. While watching the movie, the thought occurred to me, *God could have accomplished the same thing a variety of different ways.* What I mean is: *God could have chosen several different paths bringing them to the same outcome*. If I were God, here's a few ways I would have done it:

The Freeze Tag Method

Instead of sending ten plagues, God could have *tagged* all the Egyptians as in a game of freeze tag, turning them into statues while the children of Israel robbed them blind and made off with all the plunder they could gather. They could have easily skipped town, going a different way and avoiding the whole Red Sea affair. Once they were a safe distance away, God could have said, "Game over," and all the Egyptians would return to their lives as before—of course without their Israeli slaves. Or for that matter, God could have just left them frozen so Israel would never have to worry about Egypt again. That sounds much easier, wouldn't you say?

Memory Lapse Method

One morning when all of Egypt woke up, God could have simply reprogrammed their brains, exchanging their memories with the Israelites. Instead of waking up to rule the land, they would have wakened to begin a day's work in the projects. Israel could have slept in a little and rose to find the Egyptians doing all the work.

Can you imagine how Israel would have felt? "Oh, goodie! I've got the whip now. You're going to pay for the way you've treated us all these years." That would be a pretty cool way to do it! Israel wouldn't necessarily have had to leave. They could have just taken over Egypt.

The Transport Method

Have you ever seen Star Trek? I think God has. Do you remember in the New Testament when Philip was transported supernaturally from one place to another? In this case, God could have done the same thing. Israel could've simply said, "Beam us up, God!" One minute they would be in Egypt and the next moment inside the walls of Jericho to take the city. Much, much easier than walking around the city thirteen times, wouldn't you say?

A Heart Matter

You must remember that God's ultimate purpose in bringing Israel out of Egypt was not to take them to the Promised Land. *What?* That almost sounds sacrilegious, doesn't it? And yes, that was a part of the plan, but not His divine purpose. How do I know? Every account when Moses would ask Pharaoh to let his people go, he always said, "Let My people go...so that they may worship Me" (Exod 8:20). This communicated God's true desire. It was more than just taking them to the Promised Land. And that explains why they first went to Mount Sinai—to worship Him.

God's main motive was to possess a chosen people who would trust Him as their God—a peculiar people with His heartbeat. He would be their God, and they would be His people. And there was a very specific process God was taking the nation of Israel through to prepare their hearts for the Promised Land. Simply getting to it from Egypt was the easy part. The more I read through the account of Israel's deliverance from Egypt, I can't help but marvel at how God used things such as the ten plagues to not only harden Pharaoh's heart, but also capture the heart of Israel.

God's Heartbeat

Israel had just witnessed several of the most miraculous events this world has ever known: the ten plagues, a pillar of fire, and the parting of the Red Sea. Next, God led them to Mount Sinai to instruct them further in His ways. Then their so-called leader took off, saying, "Wait here. I'll see you in a couple...uh...well, I don't know how long it will be...but, I'll be back later" (see Exod 24:12-18).

It's kind of the same thing that happened to David when the leading prophet in the nation came to his hometown asking to see his father. He wasn't even invited to the dinner to welcome their guest, but God made sure he was included before all was said and done. Then the most amazing thing happened: Samuel anointed him—the little shepherd boy who wasn't important enough to get invited—as the next king of Israel. Soon afterward, the prophet left, and I can imagine hearing Jesse say, "All right David, the party's over—now get back to the sheep!" (see 1 Sam 16:19).

The same thing happened when Jesus amazingly appeared to the disciples after they had, just days before, seen Him crucified with their own eyes. They were shocked, but at the same time excited, thinking: *Finally! Now is the time we really get started at proclaiming Jesus as the gloriously risen Messiah!* Yet, shortly afterwards, He took them all to a nearby mountaintop and then floated off into the sky—leaving them again (see Acts 2:7-9). The poor disciples. God took them on an emotional roller coaster ride. He's here. No wait, He's gone. He's back. No, there He goes again.

As with Israel, all these people I've mentioned had purpose. They all were called to do great exploits for God. And all these were given the same task—a task that trips up more men and women of God than any other.

Waiting.

God anointed David, yet he waited approximately sixteen years before he became king. The disciples spent three years away from everything they'd known. Then Jesus left them and told them to go and wait some more in Jerusalem for the promise.

Let's see how Israel fared:

> *When the people saw that Moses was so long in coming down from the mountain, they gathered around Aaron and said, "Come, make us gods who*

> *will go before us. As for this fellow Moses who brought us up out of Egypt, we don't know what has happened to him." (Exod 32:1-2)*

The Israelites miserably failed the waiting test by falling into idolatry. God was angry. In fact, if Moses hadn't stepped in, begging God for mercy, they would have been completely wiped off the face of the earth (see Exod 32:10-12).

What was the problem? It was the same problem many of us have today. They wanted the blessing of all the miracles but weren't willing to wait—enduring the process—until God had finished replacing their hearts with His.

The Secret of Waiting

I believe waiting is one of the greatest secrets of God's heart. Why? Because God is patient and very longsuffering. Aren't you glad He suffers long in dealing with us?

Waiting doesn't come easily. I've never woke up and thought: *You know what I feel like doing today—waiting.* I've never purposefully gone and waited in a line or sat in a doctor's office just for the fun of it. That would be ridiculous. Why? Because there's no payoff—no reward.

When it comes to waiting, many people miss the point: It's worth waiting on God because God's reward is worth waiting for. I've also learned that the longer the wait, the greater the reward. There are multiple examples of this in Scripture, but probably none more overlooked, yet profound, than that of Moses.

Scripture tells us, "Now Moses was a very humble man, more humble than anyone else on the face of the earth" (Num 12:3). I've heard people poke fun at this Scripture because Moses was the one who wrote the book of Numbers. Read the context, and I think it's safe to say that what Moses intended by this statement was far from building himself up to look like a hero. Have you ever heard someone say, "That person came from humble beginnings"? Let's look at the journey of Abraham Lincoln to gain some insight:

Defeated for legislature, 1832

Failed in business, 1833

Elected to legislature, 1834

Sweetheart (Ann Rutledge) died, 1835

Had nervous breakdown, 1836

Defeated for Speaker, 1838

Defeated for nomination for Congress, 1843

Elected to Congress, 1846

Lost re-nomination into Congress, 1848

Defeated for Senate, 1854

Defeated for nomination for Vice-President, 1856

Again defeated for Senate, 1858

Elected President, 1860[8]

As you can see, it was a thirty-year journey of major defeats and adversities until Lincoln achieved his rise to leadership. After becoming President of the United States, Abraham Lincoln made one of his most famous statements:

"God selects His own instruments, and sometimes they are queer ones; for instance, He chose me to steer the ship through a great crisis."[9]

I see Lincoln's statement as the equivalent to Moses' statement about being the humblest man on the face of the earth. The president's remarks were not made boastfully but as a result of his difficult journey. Yet for Moses, it was not thirty years of trials and adversity but eighty. Forty of those years were spent in Egypt as a Hebrew living as the adopted son of Pharaoh. Not only was his home a place of constant pressure to perform; his background was a constant source of ridicule and his upbringing plagued by controversy.

Growing up, it is believed Moses knew (to some degree) he was ordained and destined to become Israel's deliverer. His hopes were dashed, however, after taking matters into his own hands and committing murder. He then became an outlaw and fled for his life as an exile to the desert of Midian. There, he took a wife and worked for his father-in-law, Jethro, a savvy leader and businessman. It was during this forty-year period in the desert that every dream and aspiration of Moses becoming Israel's deliverer died.

After forty years in the desert as a shepherd, Moses finally received the call from God. *It wasn't until his dreams had died that he was qualified to rise and fulfill his destiny.* This long waiting period prompted Moses' response: "You have the wrong guy, God. I'm no speaker...there must be someone else!" What was God's reply? "Now that you know you're completely incapable without Me, you're the perfect candidate." In other words: "Now that your dreams are dead, I can finally move on your behalf" (see Exod 3:10).

Over Moses' lifetime, he learned that, although difficult and at times humbling, God's reward was worth the wait.

Resurrected Dreams

Most people hate being in waiting rooms. Think about it. You're at the mercy of those you're waiting on. You have to sit in a stale environment around people you don't know. The situation is out of your control. You can't make it go faster. All you can do is sit and think about all the things you could be doing instead.

Whether your dream is success in business or ministry, or even becoming a great father, mother, husband, or wife, your dream must be submitted to God and His timetable. *Throughout Scripture, waiting is a secret tool God uses to find out whether our plans belong to us—or Him.*

I wonder if Mary and Martha felt Jesus had forgotten them when their brother Lazarus was sick and at the point of death? They sent for Jesus with plenty of time to respond and come heal Lazarus. Yet, for whatever reason, Jesus didn't come. Instead, to the surprise of His disciples, Jesus lingered where He was, and even visited another town before responding to their request.

When Jesus arrived, Mary ran out to meet Him and cried, "If you had been here, my brother would not have died" (John 11:21). Can you sense the lack of faith in her voice? It's almost as if Jesus confirmed the finality of her brother's death when He sat and wept with her. What an odd response. Jesus sat with her and cried knowing full well that Lazarus was going to be raised. What astounding compassion!

It isn't until Mary and Martha believed there was no hope of restoring the situation that Jesus stepped in and did the impossible: Lazarus was raised to life. They learned God's plan is definitely worth the wait.

One chapter later, we get a small glimpse into why Jesus didn't come right away and heal Lazarus. This Scripture also shows us a secret of God's power to sustain a resurrected dream:

> *Meanwhile a large crowd of Jews found out that Jesus was there and came, not only because of Him but also to see Lazarus, whom He had raised from the dead. So the chief priests made plans to kill Lazarus as well, for on account of him many of the Jews were going over to Jesus and believing in Him. (John 12:9-11)*

Based on this passage, we discover how profound an impact Lazarus's being raised from the dead had on the city—both positively and negatively. Large crowds that had heard Lazarus was dead (and possibly even attended his funeral) now saw him alive. After the miracle, the evidence of Jesus' being the Messiah was overwhelming, and many were putting their faith in Him. Another byproduct of the miracle wasn't so positive; the chief priests were furious.

How is this Scripture important to the waiting process? It's simple. Jesus saw the big picture. It was only by His delay that Lazarus died and all hope was lost. And it was only after he was four days in the tomb that Jesus raised him from the grave.

Ponder the Scripture again for a minute. We know the chief priests made plans to kill Jesus. But, it also says, "The chief priests made plans to kill Lazarus as well" (v. 11).

This is not a trick question, but answer this: Did the chief priests succeed in killing Jesus? The answer is yes. The more important question as it pertains to God's ability to resurrect and sustain dreams: Did the chief priests succeed in killing Lazarus? The answer is no!

Here lies the secret of waiting: *Once God resurrects your dreams, no man, demon, power in high places, family member, naysayer, government official, court system—nobody—can take it from you!*

They succeeded in their plan to kill Jesus on a cross because that was Jesus' destiny. But, when it came to Lazarus, their plans could not succeed because Lazarus was protected under the covering of Almighty God. Isn't it nice to know that Jesus' words hold a weight and authority Satan cannot penetrate? Once you've endured the waiting process and God resurrects your dreams, they are secure!

Walk On

There's one thing to keep in mind when in the waiting process: *Waiting rooms are meant to be temporary environments.* What I mean is, you're not meant to live there. In the Twenty-third Psalm, David cries out to God: "Yea, though I walk through the valley of the shadow of death" (v. 4).

Notice David says, "walk"—not sit, stand, or camp.

When they find themselves in a valley, a lot of people bring along their camping gear. While in the waiting room, one of the smartest things you'll ever do is take all that camping gear you've collected, build a big bonfire, and burn it. That's what Elisha did when he was anointed by Elijah. That's what the disciples did when Jesus asked them to leave their nets and follow Him. And when it comes to our dreams, there will be moments where God tells us, "Step out on the water and walk to Me."

Are you in the waiting room? Remember that you're on God's calendar. Also remember that waiting won't last forever—it's temporary. And, most importantly, do what David did when in the valley of the shadow of death—walk on!

CHAPTER 7

Secret of Receiving Instruction

WHAT KINDS OF PEOPLE in the world today have the hardest hearts? Think about it a minute: Is it atheists? Maybe abortionists? Perhaps homosexuals? Or could it be Satan worshipers? As much as these are easily identified as being hard-hearted, I think a different group of people are the most hard-hearted. Sadly, I've found the hardest hearts in the world today are inside the church walls.

I used to have a drama/dance group I took out on ministry trips. On one particular occasion, we had the opportunity to minister at a youth convention. After the service, a youth pastor came up to me to set me straight on some things. "Dancing is not of God," he said sternly. He went on and on about how we mustn't allow worldly things into our sacred assemblies.

In reply, I tried to explain we were only there because the pastor had invited us. Everything I said seemed to go in one ear and out the other. He was set in his beliefs and wouldn't listen with any amount of reason. After getting cut off several times, I finally stuck out my hand said, “God bless you.” Then I walked off. This was not the first time I’ve encountered someone with a hardened heart in the church.

Do you want to know the thing that’s most frustrating about this story? Later I found out that, after our time of ministry, two young people from his youth group came to the altar to accept Christ. Yet, amazingly, because of his hardened heart for the method of our presentation, he missed what God was doing right in front of his eyes.

We must be careful whenever we hold the perspective, “This is the way it is, and I don’t care what you say; I’m not changing.” This attitude is a sure sign of one thing: a hardened heart.

Jesus’ Ministry

Have you ever wondered why Jesus was called *a friend of sinners*? It is amazing to me how Jesus was drawn to those everyone else ignored. One day he walked into a city and spotted a man perched in a tree who everyone else overlooked. Jesus stopped the caravan and called out to Zacchaeus, “Come down…I’m staying at your house tonight.” The proof of Zacchaeus’s conversion is evident when he (on his own accord) declared, “I will stop cheating people and return four times what I’ve stolen” (see Luke 19:5, 8).

Here’s what people—church people, mind you—said about Jesus staying at the tax collector’s house: “Here is a glutton and a drunkard, a friend of tax collectors and sinners” (Matt 11:19).

More hard hearts in the church.

The same attitude is seen when Jesus is anointed by a sinful woman. She anointed His feet with perfume and tears, then wiped them with her hair. As she did, there was an indignant attitude in the room from the religious leader in whose house they sat as well as from Jesus' own disciples. What did He do? Jesus rebuked them. That's right, Jesus rebuked those in the church and embraced the sinful woman, calling her *blessed*.

This is only a matter of opinion, but some believe this event was the defining moment when Judas, who was keeper of the moneybag, said, "What a waste," and decided to betray Jesus. Neither he nor the religious leader understood how precious this single act of worship meant to the Son of God.

More hard hearts in the church.

Jesus was known for loving the worst of society—the gangsters, the prostitutes, the cheaters and thieves. But, you know the one group that Jesus had no mercy on? Those in the church—the scribes, Pharisees, and Sadducees. Here's what He said about them on one occasion:

> *Woe to you, teachers of the law and Pharisees, you hypocrites! You are like whitewashed tombs, which look beautiful on the outside but on the inside are full of the bones of the dead and everything unclean. (Matt 23:27)*

Godly Instruction

Satan loves people who can't admit they're wrong. These people become like islands out on the ocean, isolated from a world filled with wonder and knowledge. Proverbs 11:14 says, "Where no counsel is the people fall: but in the multitude of counsel there is safety." Notice how the meek man Moses was able to accept the wise counsel of his father-in-law Jethro (see Exod 18:13-27). He not only accepted it, he acted on it!

In all the years I did college ministry, I was fascinated by this one fatal flaw of those in the age bracket: Many of them had an extremely hard time accepting counsel from other people such as parents, family, and friends. Even now, it seems crazy to me that, at an age when people are making the most important decisions of their lives, they are the least teachable. Think about it: In their early twenties, most people decide what they're going to do in life, who they're going to marry, where and how they're going to live. And yet, at that age, many are unwilling to receive wise counsel.

What's tragic is, I've sat across from many in their thirties and forties and counseled them through the bad decisions of their twenties. Many are going through their first or second divorce. A lot are in deep debt, addicted to different substances or hiding in secret sins, and trying to salvage what's left.

Here's the good news: *The secret heart of God is to restore those most wounded and broken.* God's grace and mercy is the only thing that can piece a torn life back together and make it new again.

With that said, there are some life decisions that take a longer time to mend. Why? Because our decisions don't just affect us but the people around us. The damage inflicted on our kids, family members, spouses, or friends can sometimes take a lifetime to heal. And yet, the more we humble ourselves, the more hope there is for healing to take place.

These are two of the most depressing Scriptures in the Bible. But they give us a glimpse of why some have ended up in such dark and desperate places: "Therefore, he who rejects instruction does not reject man but God, who gives you his Holy Spirit" (1 Thess 4:8). Even more alarming is the following: "Whoever remains stiff-necked after many rebukes will suddenly be destroyed—without remedy" (Prov 29:1).

These verses warn us of God's judgment on those who won't accept instruction. When those far from God, such as drug addicts, prostitutes, or atheists, receive a true taste of God's love and compassionate heart for them, they will respond. I've seen it. Even the hardest of hearts becomes soft and pliable under the convicting power of the Holy Spirit.

There is a danger, however, for those sitting in the church who hear God's Word week after week yet do not respond with action. Each week, their hearts become a little less pliable. *I've found there's only one kind of person God cannot help: those unwilling to accept His help.*

Are You Teachable?

There is another term God uses to describe the hard-hearted. It is only used one time in the entire Bible. In Revelation 3:15-16, the Lord spoke to the church of Laodicea, saying: "You are neither cold nor hot, I wish you were either one or the other! So, because you are lukewarm—neither hot nor cold—I am about to spit you out of My mouth."

How does one become lukewarm? A few short verses later God says, "Those whom I love I rebuke and discipline" (Rev 3:19). Ask the children of Israel about rebuke and discipline. All you have to do is flip open any one of the Old Testament prophetic books such as Isaiah, Jeremiah, or Ezekiel and read a few excerpts. Israel never seemed to learn their lesson. God gave them chance after chance, but they refused to take heed. And time after time, after not receiving His discipline, they were judged and handed over to their enemies.

On a hot muggy day, after working outside, doesn't a nice lukewarm glass of water sound refreshing? On a cold day, doesn't a mug of lukewarm coffee sound good? Of course not! Neither does lukewarm lasagna or salmon sound appetizing when you're hungry. Yuck!

Lukewarm Christians upset God's stomach. He can't digest them. Their hearts are too hard. In fact, based on John's account of the church of Laodicea, we learn He prefers the atheist above the half-committed believer.

If refusing the Lord's rebuke leads to a lukewarm existence, I wonder why it is hard to accept His discipline?

Contrary to popular opinion, not everything God has to say to us is pleasurable at the time. We love when God speaks about blessing and prosperity but tend to turn up our nose when He asks us to sacrifice or give up something. This is one reason I believe fasting is almost a non-existent aspect in many churches today.

When God speaks to us about pushing away from the table and going to our knees, right away we assume: *That wasn't God; that was just me.* Chances are—if it drives you to give up something, sacrifice of yourself, or go to your knees—it's God. In fact, to my knowledge, I've never waken up in the morning and thought: *You know what I feel like doing today—fasting.*

I'm quite convinced many Christians today don't *apply* certain aspects from the Word of God because those aspects don't *appeal* to them. Growing up, when my mom placed a pile of green beans on my plate, I had to eat them. Not just the sweets. Not just the bread or meat, but the greens. Job said, "Shall we receive only pleasant things from the hand of God and never anything unpleasant?" (Job 2:10 TLB).

It's impossible to grow healthy and strong without a balanced diet of the whole counsel of God. We can't accept certain aspects of God's character and reject others. Here's a good description of godly discipline:

> *Those whom I love I rebuke and discipline. So be earnest, and repent. Here I am! I stand at the door and knock. If anyone hears My voice and opens the door, I will come in and eat with him, and he with Me. (Rev 3:19-20)*

As much as rebuke and discipline are difficult, this verse makes it clear—it is necessary. *And here's the great news: After rebuke comes intimacy.* Every time I discipline one of my children, I always hold them in my arms and affirm them of my love.

If the hardest hearts tend to be in the church, how do we keep our hearts soft and pliable? I'll pose the secret as a question, or more of a challenge: Are you teachable? In John's words: Are you open to the Lord's rebuke and discipline?

I've found those with soft and pliable hearts who heed rebuke live victorious Christian lives—closely intimate with their heavenly Father. When God stands and knocks on the door of our hearts, we must answer. The outcome: God will come in and sit and eat with, be intimate with, and reveal Himself to those who will accept His instruction. What an invitation!

The Man's Man

I hope you're familiar with the phrase the "man's man." If not, let me describe him to you. We've all seen him. He walks around with his chest flared and fists clenched. Plastered on his face is the brazen look of a tough guy. Typically, you see him standing around outside of bars, possibly smoking a cigarette and sporting a beer. He can also be seen looking all tough in the weight room, chumming around with the guys at work, strutting down the street and the aisle in the church. *What?* Did I say *the church*?

Yeah, I see him walk in the back door of church all the time. I can recognize him almost immediately by the way he walks, greets people, and carries himself. It becomes more apparent during worship as his face and body language show signs of his discomfort. I admit it's almost amusing to watch.

A man's man stands up straight as a board with a staunch look on his face. He doesn't have his right hand on his brow as if saluting an officer. But, if you can envision, it's the same body posture, probably more like when a drill sergeant says, "At ease, men!" That "at ease" posture, for lack of a better term, is exactly how a man's man looks standing in a congregation full of vibrant worshipers. While others have hands raised and expressive faces of adoration, the man's man stands like a pillar—never flinching, with hands tightly held one over the other at belt buckle level. No matter what song is being sung, all the man's man can hear is the words of an old hymn, "I shall not be...I shall not be moved!"

Like me, maybe you wonder, *Is this just an act he puts on when people are around?* Truthfully, I'm not sure. I would assume that in the privacy of his home, the man's man relaxes and lightens up like the average guy. But, who knows, maybe he's tough all the time. Regardless, I hope you will agree there's something desperately wrong with this picture.

Why does a man's man feel the need to put on the macho mask?

First of all, a man's man doesn't put on his own mask. It's put on by others who wear the mask themselves or those who grew up in that environment—many times by a father, mother, step father, or whoever raised the man's man. It is transferred through statements like, "Now, you listen here, stand up and take it like a man," or, "Don't let me catch you crying. Men don't cry!" These cause a boy or young man to stiffen up, bury his feelings, and block all emotions from the world.

Secondly, after being belittled time and time again, a man's man begins to carry the mask around wherever he goes, wearing it more and more frequently as circumstances call for it. Before long, the mask becomes a permanent way of life. His emotions get locked up in a bolted trunk buried deep within his soul.

A Broken Lock

One Sunday morning, I watched as Bill came walking through the back door of the church. Why did I notice? Because Bill was a man's man who, for some reason, piqued my interest. He usually came in late and left early, avoiding contact with people in the church. This Sunday, however, would prove to be far different.

In worship, God's presence was undeniably strong. At the end of it, a call was given for the men of our church to rise and be delivered of weights and set free from bondage. It was spontaneous, and as I looked out over the congregation, I could see men all over being stirred by the Spirit of God. Some were praying with their heads down, others were crying, and then there was Bill—standing like a statue in his "at ease" military pose.

I could sense that the Holy Spirit was working on him. It's hard to explain what I saw, but I would liken it to a pot of water on a hot burner getting ready to boil over. It was as if, from that dull straight-ahead stare, he was calling out, "Somebody please help me! I'm trapped in here, and I can't get out!" For what seemed like an eternity he wouldn't move—not one little budge. That is, until...it happened—Bill exploded!

To my surprise, in a brisk walk, from the back right-hand side of the church, Bill came charging up to the front and stood at the altar. Almost instantly, men from all over the building followed in his footsteps. Bill stood directly in front of me, and I watched him closely. Granted, he was still standing at attention, but I could see big tears rolling down both sides of his cheeks. On occasion, he would reach a hand to wipe them away but then put it right back down to his belt buckle.

Bill must have cried for twenty straight minutes. Several times it was an uncontrollable cry. As I watched him weep, I could imagine the burdens of pain and heaviness he'd carried for years being lifted. It was a glorious sight.

I was curious and later found Bill and asked him what had happened. He shared with me about his difficult background—growing up in an abusive home with no father. As he talked, he kept fighting back the tears. He went on to explain how it felt like weights coming off his shoulders as he wept at the altar.

In the years to come, I saw a very different Bill. He was no longer hard and calloused, yet neither was he soft and mushy. He was as tough a man as I've ever met—but different. God broke the padlock of pride and opened the trunk deep within Bill's soul, pouring tears of healing balm onto an otherwise hardened man.

God has used my experience with knowing Bill in ways I never imagined. I've shared it with many men who are hesitant to lay down their pride and give God a chance to heal deep emotional wounds, and watched as God did the same for them.

Hope for the Man's Man

I've encountered thousands upon thousands of tough guys just like Bill. On the outside, they have your typical macho demeanor, but on the inside they're crying out for a different life. They are exhausted from being tough. They are sick and tired of not buckling when all hell is breaking loose around them. Sometimes it takes everything they've got to hold up the wall of isolation to the outside world. Inside they are dying, but the padlock of pride just seems too thick to break asunder. Guys like Bill, if they don't reach out, end up living lonely, miserable, and defeated Christian lives.

In his book, *Tender Warrior*, Stu Weber wrote the following about one of America's finest Generals, Norman Schwarzkopf:

"Not long after the Gulf War and dazzling victory over Iraq, the conquering commander of Desert Storm appeared on national television in an interview with Barbara Walters. In the course of their conversation about the war, something touched the big man. We all watched with fascination as the eyes of this career soldier with four stars on his shoulder glazed over. Tears formed. Ms. Walters, with well-practiced bluntness, said, 'Why, General, aren't you afraid to cry?' Stormin' Norman replied without hesitation, 'No, Barbara. I'm afraid of a man who won't cry!'"[10]

There's one thing I've noticed about the man's man. Although he's been trained to hold his emotions in, they end up coming out anyway—in other forms. Have you ever wondered why Uncle Bob never cried when Aunt Julie died, but often gets in fits of drunken rage, throwing temper tantrums and hitting walls? Why is it that daddy will stand reverently in worship services only to get upset after church and curse at mommy? Why is it that so many dads become workaholics under the excuse, "I've got to provide for my family, don't I?"

Anger, bitterness, rage, jealousy, and running away from problems, are some of the by-products of a man's man who won't release his feelings. A proud man who won't ask for help is a bitter man who suffers alone. A proud man who is too tough to cry often ends up throwing tantrums of rage. *A man's man who won't lay down his pride is not hopeless, but he is helpless!*

As long as we run away from God's love, we cannot be helped. But there is hope. Read the following Scriptures and catch a glimmer of hope from the secret heart of God. These verses contrast a proud man with a humble man of virtue. You be the judge which lifestyle God blesses:

> *Every one that is proud in heart is an abomination to the Lord: though hand join in hand, he shall not be unpunished. By mercy and truth iniquity is purged: and by the fear of the Lord men depart from evil. (Prov 16:5-6 KJV)*

> *He who is of a proud heart stirs up strife, but he who trusts in the Lord will be prospered. (Prov 28:25 NKJV)*

You notice in these two verses how pride is looked down up, yet hope and healing are also promised. Here's one more example I feel says it best:

> *Better is the end of a thing than the beginning thereof: and the patient in spirit is better than the proud in spirit. (Eccl 7:8)*

These verses unfold incredible secrets from the heart of God for the man's man. You may have been sold a bill of goods growing up. Perhaps your dad was a hard man, and he raised you to be rough and tough like he was. That proud spirit is not what God is looking for. No matter how you were raised and no matter how thick the mask you've been raised with, your upbringing doesn't have to define you.

Your end can be better than your beginning. God has a wonderful plan for your life. His plans are not to harm you but to prosper you. His plans are to give you hope and a future (read Jer 29:11). God has also promised that in our weakness He is made strong (read 2 Cor 13:10).

So stop trying to be so strong! Let Him come in and soften that hardened and calloused heart. Receive instruction from Him in all meekness. God can turn you from a man's man into His man!

CHAPTER 8

Secret of Usefulness

WHEN I WAS A BOY, I loved playing in the sandbox. In grade school, I couldn't care less about the slides, monkey bars, or swings. Isn't this a typical little boy: *Forget the clean stuff, let's get dirty!* In fact, we had a sandbox out in the backyard of our house. My favorite thing was playing with my Hot Wheels in the sandbox. I remember all my friends coming over and helping me make a Hot Wheels city. We'd build tunnels, overpasses, ramps, and everything else our little eight-year-old minds could manage to think up.

One day, we decided to add water. Big mistake! As you can imagine, before long our city had turned into one big mud pit. This was just one of our problems. The biggest was that many of our beloved Hot Wheels had been buried and lost in the mud.

We began digging, all the time getting more and more filthy. It wasn't long until all the Hot Wheels were found except one—my favorite one: *the* famous Dukes of Hazard—General Lee. Man, I loved that car! I dug and dug until it was dark. No luck! My little heart was broken as I retreated into the house. The next morning, I looked again but to no avail. My General Lee was lost.

Several months after the incident, my friends and I were out in the sandbox again. I think it was my brilliant idea, "Hey guys, let's dig a pit and see how deep we can make it!" They went along with the idea, and shortly afterwards we were knee-deep. I bet you can never guess what I found—the General Lee. But, it didn't look the same any more. It had turned a rust color, and the wheels no longer rolled. It was completely useless.

A Useless Belt

Have you ever had a belt that gets so dilapidated it won't work anymore? Or how about when you're tying your shoe and the shoelace breaks? How frustrating! It's better to not even try to fix it. Just buy new ones because they're no good for use. The same was true with my favorite Hot Wheels car.

Jeremiah was instructed to buy a belt and then hide it in the sand. After retrieving it months later, it had become just like my General Lee. It was good for nothing but the scrap heap. It was completely useless.

> *This is what the Lord said to me: "Go and buy a linen belt and put it around your waist, but do not let it touch water...." Then the word of the Lord came a second time: "Take the belt you bought and are wearing around your waist, and go to Perath and hide it there in a crevice in the rocks...." Many days later the Lord said to me, "Go now to Perath and get the belt I told you to hide there." So I went to Perath and dug up the belt and took it from the place where I had hidden it,*

> *but now it was ruined and completely useless. Then the word of the Lord came to me: "This is what the Lord says: In the same way I will ruin the pride of Judah and the great pride of Jerusalem." (Jer 13:1-9)*

God is so loving and forgiving. He is a patient God. Every time I read through the Old Testament, I realize how many chances God gave the children of Israel to turn away from other gods and renounce their wicked ways. Time and time again, His grace and mercies were made known. But God is also a just God. There is a point when enough is enough. In this portion of Scripture, God makes it very clear what kind of judgment would come upon the great pride of Judah and Jerusalem: uselessness.

Useless Tools

There's nothing more frustrating than trying to complete a task with either the wrong tool or a tool that won't work anymore. Recently, I landscaped my backyard. I called up a friend that knew something about landscaping and asked him to help me put in sprinklers. He assured me that it would take about two days. The following Saturday morning, we went down to Home Depot and bought all the supplies. Now, of course, being the thrifty person that I am, I decided to cut corners a little. Instead of buying the expensive twenty-five-dollar pipe cutters, I bought the cheapie eight-dollar pipe cutters.

To make a long story short, a two-day job turned into a two-week job. The pipe cutters kept slipping and wouldn't cut. They broke the pipes half the time. And of course, since I had already invested a whopping eight-dollars in them, I wasn't going to go back and spend another twenty-five for a good pair. It was the longest two weeks of my life. Just two words of advice if you're putting in sprinklers: Buy good pipe cutters and rent a trencher instead of digging the trenches all with a shovel.

I've seen people that have all the right talents and abilities for God to use them. Yes, they put themselves in the hand of God. But often, like my cheap pipe cutters, whenever He goes to use them they refuse to cut, or they break down because they don't think God is doing the right procedure.

If we would trust that God knows what He's doing, our two-day tasks wouldn't turn into two-week, two-year, or twenty-year tasks.

If He wants us to love the seemingly unlovable, fine. If He wants us to feed the homeless, fine. If He wants us to minister to our angry neighbor, fine. If He wants us to clean toilets, let's do it with a cheerful heart. Why? Because God knows what He's doing. We can trust Him! There's too much to be done for the kingdom of God to become useless.

When it comes to trusting in God's plan, here's another important thought to consider: Are you the right tool for the job? If God called me to stop being in front and leading worship or speaking, I would. In fact, I wish during the worship time, the worship leader and musicians could be in the balcony or behind the congregation. I've often said, "Our presence on stage is the biggest distraction to His presence."

What task has God called you to do? Wouldn't it be tragic to be in a position someone else could do better or more effectively for the Kingdom? I've heard of successful singers that, late in their careers, admit God's initial call was not singing but something else. How tragic! Just think what God could have accomplished through them had they trusted in His plan.

What kind of a tool are you? Are you trying to work your way into the spotlight as a worship leader, preacher, musician, teacher, or business leader, when God has called you to do something else? Now let's turn that around: Are you supposed to be a leader but refuse to obey? Are you saying, "I'll let someone else do it; they don't need me"?

Terry Nance said this:

"Never be too big to do the little things, and never be too little to do the big things."[10]

Just as Satan's secret of I caused Israel to become useless in God's hand, when we are out of position, we fall into the same trap. Regardless of what you may think or have been told, God needs you! He needs everyone to find their respective places in the body of Christ.

God and Numbers

As I think about the tragedy of uselessness, I can't help but wonder what is the cause. Certainly being out of position can stifle a person's effectiveness. As we will discuss more fully in a future chapter, sometimes success can be a culprit. Even rejection can play a role. And yet, I find a surprising trend that Satan is using to render God's people useless: numbers.

I know God is somewhat concerned about numbers. If not, He wouldn't have entitled a chapter in His book *Numbers*. Additionally, throughout Scripture, numbers are mentioned. Jesus fed five thousand men with five loaves and two fish. Peter preached on the Day of Pentecost, and three thousand were saved at one time. Face this fact: We will always have to deal with numbers. But we mustn't let numbers determine our level of success.

Jesus ministered to the masses, but the majority of His time was spent with twelve grumbling, complaining menaces to society. Jesus was also quick to go out of His way to reach one or two: the woman at the well, blind Bartimaeus, Philip, Matthew, Zacchaeus, and many more.

I've noticed the attitude is very much alive in many churches: *If I'm not asked to do something great, I'm not doing anything at all.* Oh, it's never verbalized, but it's there. I've thought it myself. *God, You wouldn't ask me, the worship leader, to mow the grass, clean the toilets, or vacuum. God, You wouldn't ask me to go to lunch with that person after church. God, You wouldn't ask me to drive three hours one way to minister to that Bible study group of forty people.* All the while God's saying, "Yes, I would—now get busy!"

Nobody wants to admit it, but there are times we think (subconsciously) we're too good for a particular task. Without ever saying a word, our attitude displays disgust when asked to do a menial task or minister to a small crowd.

If you're in ministry, ask yourself this question every now and again: Do I prepare to minister the same when there are twenty people as opposed to two hundred or two thousand? I guarantee Jesus and the apostles did!

Opposition

When I was young, I liked to play with magnets. Now these weren't the typical magnets we stick on refrigerator doors. These were solid steel and the size of a horseshoe.

We all know that in order for magnets to stick together, you have to put the positive end with the negative and vice versa. But that's boring. The fun was trying to put the positive with the positive. My friends and I would get down on the floor, two or three on each side and see how close we could get the two magnets together. We'd brace ourselves every way imaginable and push and pull with all our might. Putting one magnet up against the wall, we'd take a running start sliding across the floor only to get thrown back. No matter how hard we tried, we could never get the two magnets together.

The final stages of Satan's secret of I are like those magnets. God and a prideful person simply cannot come together. Not only can they not come together, there's an incredible force pushing them apart. They are going in completely different directions. Jeremiah 13:15-17 says:

> *"Hear and pay attention, do not be arrogant, for the Lord has spoken. Give glory to the Lord your God before he brings the darkness, before your feet stumble on the darkened hills. You hope for light, but he will turn it to thick darkness and change it to deep gloom. But if you do not listen, I will weep in secret because of your pride."*

Many of the sins we commit as human beings have a natural progression leading to punishment. As a child I was told, "If you play, you've got to pay." If you steal, cheat, and lie, there will be punishment. If you murder, you may go to prison or even be put to death. If you cheat on your taxes, there will be legal consequences. If you go into deep debt, you'll find yourself enslaved to creditors.

But think about if someone sinned—they lied or fornicated—and were never caught and never received punishment. Many men addicted to pornography think to themselves: *It doesn't hurt anybody but myself.* Closet alcoholics think the same kinds of thought: *I hold a steady job, and I only drink in my room at night when no one's around. I only do it because it helps me relax and go to sleep.*

These are exactly the secrets Satan wants us to embrace. Even if you never get caught and never suffer earthly consequence, God sees. For those bound by Satan's secret of I this is a scary verse: "God opposes the proud but shows favor to the humble" (Jas 4:6). You notice it's not Satan who's bringing opposition. We have to realize, destruction of the proud doesn't come from Satan; it comes from God.

Few times in this book will I be so direct. But here it goes. Please, don't be prideful. Please, deal with those hidden—secret—sins. Why? Because God cannot break His promises! Not only will you squelch your spiritual growth and effectiveness, rendering yourself useless, you will literally find yourself fighting against God. Trust me when I say that God never loses. No matter how hard you try, you'll find yourself on the other end of the magnet wearing yourself out.

Do you ever feel like everything you try fails? Does it seem like you reach a certain level in God and can't seem to go any further? Maybe the same is true in your ministry? When life gets too hard and you find yourself in the same predicament time and time again, maybe it's time to ask, "Is there any pride in me?"

James 1:5 says, "If any of you lacks wisdom, he should ask God, who gives generously to all without finding fault, and it will be given to him." David said it this way, "Search me, God, and know my heart; test me and know my anxious thoughts. See if there is any offensive way in me, and lead me in the way everlasting" (Ps 139:23-24).

Ask God what the problem is. If there's a hidden pride issue there, He'll expose it to you. Better to have Him expose it to you in private than to all in public, don't you think?

I failed to mention one crucial fact about the magnets. When you flip the magnets around, they will quickly come together—making it difficult to pull them apart. James describes it this way, "Draw nigh unto God, and He will draw nigh unto you" (Jas 4:7-10). Just as God opposes the proud, when they turn it around and do the opposite, He will give grace and favor to the humble (Jas 4:6).

A Prodigal Returns

When I was doing college ministry, my wife and I made it a point to pray for a young lady who was extremely troubled. We knew she was going through something but didn't feel the liberty to approach her about it. So we waited. One week, unexpectedly, she showed up to one of our Friday night prayer groups.

At one point, we went around the group, and each person shared how he or she was doing and then presented any prayer needs. When it was her turn, she started to talk and immediately broke down crying. "I've been having a really hard time the last six months," she shared. "But, this week, God revealed to me I'd put a relationship with a boy in front of my relationship with Him. I've been running from God ever since only to become heartbroken." Now sobbing, she said, "I want to come back to God and get involved with the church again."

I asked her to stand and come to the middle of the room so we could pray for her. As we gathered around her and prayed, the Holy Spirit spoke to my heart. I silenced the prayer group and asked her to look at me and then shared with her what God had showed me. "Anytime we run away from God," I said, "our natural tendency is to think: *I've run from God for the last six months, now it's going to take me just as long to turn and run back into His arms.* Yet, because of His marvelous grace, as soon as we turn around, we find Jesus there with open arms. He'd been following us all along."

That very night, she ended the relationship that was pulling her away from God. In the months ahead, I saw a radical change in her life. She was joyful and began serving in the church again. A few years later, God also brought a wonderful man along whom she married that loved God as much as she did. Today, they are both still serving in the church.

The truth is, no matter how long we've been serving God, in one way or another we all have pride. We all are prodigals. We all have times of running from God and doing our own thing. Like this precious young lady, those who humble themselves and deal with their pride will be equipped and strengthened by God. *Only God has the ability to turn something useless into something useful!*

CHAPTER 9

Secret of Thankfulness & More

I GREW UP IN A FAMILY with three growing boys. My cousin also lived with us from the time I was six on up to college. With five guys (including my dad) in the house, there was one thing we knew how to do—eat!

On Thanksgiving at our house, we not only thanked God for all He'd done throughout the year, we also ate tremendous amounts of delicious food. My mom is a wonderful cook. She'd go out of her way to make everything exactly the way we liked it. In fact, I remember a few days before Thanksgiving, she'd get each of our orders on sweets. By the time Thanksgiving rolled around, each one had his favorite dessert prepared for after the feast. It was awesome!

There was only one problem. Most of the time, we'd all be so full by the end of Thanksgiving dinner, we didn't have any room for dessert. Sometimes we'd cram it in anyway only to feel sick the rest of the day. But, hey, that's what Thanksgiving is all about, right? You eat yourself silly 'til you're completely satisfied, right?

The Israelites had the same problem. God said about them: "When I fed them, they were satisfied. When they were satisfied, they became proud; then they forgot me" (Hos 13:6).

Unfortunately, I believe this prophecy is still as alive and well today as it was the moment Hosea first declared it.

It's interesting that Hosea was not speaking to Israel's poverty but to their prosperity. No one becomes satisfied with poverty. No one grows satisfied in the midst of adversity or trials. Like on Thanksgiving Day, satisfaction comes from being fed and nourished well. Most of the time, it's not in the bad times you need to worry about Satan's secret of I; it's in the good times.

A Prophecy, a House, and a Praise

I have to admit I've had times of blessing from the Lord that have blown my mind. One such time, my wife and I were given a prophetic word. The man said: "God is going to surround you with a dwelling place. Everything is going to fall into place. In fact, it's already in the making as I speak."

Little did this man know we had been praying for a year about buying a new house. The next day, I had an appointment with a realtor (which I had previously made) to look into our options.

The prophetic word was on target because everything fell into place just as the man had said. A few hours after the appointment that day, we were reserving a lot in a small town nearby that we had our eye on. The house we qualified for was a little smaller than we hoped for, but since we were young and it was our first house, we figured we could make do.

The next day, we went back to look at the model homes in our future development and walked into the house one step larger than ours. I remember thinking: *Boy, this would be perfect. This is what we really need.* Not wanting to be ungrateful, I didn't say anything. I was settled on being satisfied with the smaller house.

Two days later, the realtor called me up saying, "I just had a cancellation on a house. It's the only one like this we have left. It's a little bigger than the one you were looking at, but I think we can stretch your money to make it work if you're interested. Oh, and, the good news is, it's halfway built and you can be in it by Thanksgiving" (which was four weeks away).

I bet you can never guess which house he was talking about? The one I'd secretly hoped for. As I thought about the prophetic word we'd received, I remembered he'd said, "It's already in the making as I speak."

Come to find out, we qualified—barely. The house had just reached the construction stage before all the colors were selected, so we were able to pick out everything we wanted. Also, they threw in a free fireplace and electrical package—a two-thousand-dollar value. Plus, we were in before the holidays. Four weeks later, we sat there in our empty house during Thanksgiving as happy as could be—smiles from ear to ear.

On Thanksgiving night, my wife and I sat in the living room, and I had such a strong urge to praise and thank God. We kneeled down on the floor and began to sing and praise Him for this blessing. I'm not talking about a little half-hearted song to the Lord; we sang from the depths of our souls. And as we did, God's glory filled the room.

At one point, I turned to my wife and said, “We can never, ever stop thanking God for His blessings.” I said it, I meant it, and we did it. After a long while thanking and praising God that night, God spoke to me and said, *“Thanksgiving is the path to continual blessing.”*

Without knowing it at the time, that night I discovered a secret in the heart of God. Think about it. How apt are you to give a gift to someone who isn’t thankful? Why would God bless us further if we weren’t thankful for the blessings we already had received?

That night I made a conscious decision to be thankful, and because of this powerful secret in God’s heart, I’ve seen continual blessing through the years.

Too many times, when God’s blessing comes, our priorities get mixed up. Our focus begins to shift from God to our own accomplishments. How easily I could have thought, *Well, I am only twenty-two years old, but I do have a college degree and have saved a good chunk of money. I’ve put in the effort, so it was bound to happen eventually.* If that were true, and I had done it my way, I would have ended up with a smaller house or perhaps even with no house at all. Without God’s favor, who is to say what might have happened.

Nine Unthankful Lepers

The Bible speaks about a time when Jesus healed ten lepers. Now, you must understand, lepers were social outcasts who lived in a segregated colony outside the city, away from family and friends. This was law because leprosy is contagious. Once it was confirmed that you had the disease, it wasn’t an issue of discussion. You were required to pack your bags and get out. Once banished, you didn’t return—ever! People were not kind to lepers;

they were afraid of them. They didn't want to take any chance of getting the horrible disease. As you can imagine, it was not a laughing matter if a leper wandered into town.

This group of ten lepers did everything required to receive a miracle. They took a step of faith by coming in a little too close to town (risking death) and seeking the healer they'd heard about. They sought God, were desperate for His touch, and because of their bold faith, God blessed them with Jesus' words, "Go, show yourselves to the priests" (Luke 17:14). As they went, they were cleansed. What a wonderful story! Jesus healed them—everything was great, right?

This story does not have a happy ending, however. The Bible says, "One of them, when he saw he was healed, came back, praising God in a loud voice. He threw himself at Jesus' feet and thanked Him—and he was a Samaritan" (Luke 17:15). Only one of the ten came back giving Jesus the proper thanks. Statistically, that's only 10%!

Could it be God is making a point here that He's not receiving enough thanksgiving from His blessings? Also, you may note, this man was a Samaritan—not a Jew. "Jesus asked, 'Were not all ten cleansed? Where are the other nine? Was no one found to return and give praise to God except this foreigner?'" (Luke 17:17-18).

God's Expectation

Can you read between the lines here? Jesus is appalled, utterly shocked that these other nine Jews ran off without thanking Him. The only one who returned was a Samaritan. Can you hear the surprise in Jesus' voice? He can't believe it. Why? Here's the secret: Jesus expected to be thanked for what He'd done!

What happened to the other nine? Perhaps they were so caught up in fulfilling the proper religious routine in front of the priests they forgot to stop and say *thank you*. Jesus went on to tell the man, "Rise and go; your faith has made you well" (Luke 17:19). You notice, He said nothing to the man about showing himself to the priest the second time. He just said, "Go."

Who knows what the reason for the oversight. Perhaps they didn't know or just plain forgot. Whatever the reason, it's undeniable our flesh easily gets distracted in the midst of God's blessing. This story is not noted for its faith aspect but as a warning to those God has blessed.

Take another look at the prophet Hosea's words: "When I fed them, they were satisfied. When they were satisfied, they became proud; then they forgot Me" (Hos 13:6).

The nine lepers received what they needed at the time. But what did they miss? They ran back to their busy lives and missed being able to thank the Son of God, who was sent to redeem them from their sins. Who knows if they ever saw God's Messiah—their Savior—ever again.

Successful versus Satisfied

St. Bernard said,

"It is no great thing to be humble when you are brought low; but to be humble when you are praised is a great and rare attainment."[12]

When God's blessing comes, we must be very careful how we respond. It will make us or break us. Responding to God's blessing in the proper way is crucial to remaining successful in His eyes.

A man who walked with Jesus said, "Do not err, my beloved brethren. Every good gift and every perfect gift is from above, and cometh down from the Father of lights" (Jas 1:16-17a KJV). Success comes from the Father. Financial blessing comes from the Father. Your children are a blessing from the Father. Every breath is a blessing from the Father.

I don't care how successful you are—if you become satisfied—watch out! Don't take anything for granted. Why? In the words of the old Frank Sinatra song:

"That's life. That's what all the people say. You're riding high in April, shot down in May."[13]

Things can change in a hurry. Saul, Samson, Nebuchadnezzar, or Ahab would be great examples of how things can change dramatically when God is not given the thanks He deserves.

Judgment from Satisfaction

For the third time, read the Scripture from Hosea as well as the verses that follows:

> *"When I fed them, they were satisfied. When they were satisfied, they became proud; then they forgot Me. So I will come upon them like a lion. Like a leopard I will lurk by the path. Like a bear robbed of her cubs, I will attack them and rip them open. Like a lion I will devour them: a wild animal will tear*

them apart. You are destroyed, O Israel, against your helper." (Hos 13:7-9)

As you can see, God's response to Israel's satisfaction led to brutal ramifications. You may also notice, it wasn't the result of difficulty—but blessing. I know people extremely blessed by God who no longer feel the need to learn new things anymore. Meanwhile, their family, their ministry, or business has been at the same stagnant place it's been for the last umpteen years. They can handle it. They can control it and manage it without too much worry. They've become *satisfied*.

As you read through the Gospels, you may notice that Jesus didn't mention much about the sins of the scribes and Pharisees. He knew they had sin. He knows we all have sin issues we deal with. That's why He came.

What He did denounce was their satisfaction with the law and the things of God. Their worship was nothing more than rituals made by men. They rejoiced in their long-drawn-out prayers. They were proud of all the Scriptures they'd memorized. They were proud of how many times a week they fasted. Yet, despite their flawless routines, God no longer accepted their sacrifices.

Content not Satisfied

You may be wondering: *If I'm not to be satisfied, then what attitude am I supposed to take?* We've all heard this favorite verse of the Bible: "I can do all things through Christ which strengthens me" (Phil 4:13). This Scripture has been taken out of context for years. When put it context it gives us the secret for overcoming a satisfied life.

Here's the verse just before the famous passage:

> *I rejoiced greatly in the Lord...for I have learned to be content whatever the circumstances. I know what it is to be in need, and I know what it is to have plenty. I have learned the secret of being content in any and every situation, whether well fed or hungry, whether living in plenty or in want. I can do all things through Him who gives me strength. (Phil 4:10a-13)*

Did you catch what the author, Paul, needed strength for? It wasn't strength to conquer sin. Neither was it strength to stand against persecution (which he encountered frequently). He was asking God for strength to be "content" in every circumstance.

In the depths of God's heart, finding contentment without being satisfied is a secret few learn. Solomon is another good example of someone who was content but not satisfied. Can you imagine if God showed up at your doorstep and said, "Ask for anything you want and I'll grant it"? In Solomon's case, God sounded more like a genie in a lamp. Here was Solomon's humble reply: "Give your servant a discerning heart to govern your people and to distinguish between right and wrong. For who is able to govern this great people of yours?" (1 Kgs 3:9)

In essence, Solomon prayed, "Help!" He was certainly content in where God had placed him—as king—but not satisfied to coast on the coattails of his father David. He was in over his head, and he knew it. Like Paul, Solomon needed strength to fulfill his task. He cried out for wisdom, and God not only granted it but gave him more than he could dream or imagine.

Content with Spiritual Gifts

There are those who don't like the position in which God has placed them. They complain, "Why did You place me here? I want to be like that man or woman up there. Come on God, I'm better than this!"

We must be content with where God has placed us but never satisfied. I thank God for blessing me with a beautiful home, healthy children, and a godly wife. I thank God for what He's done through my life and ministry. But I'm not quitting. I'll never arrive. The moment I think I arrive in any area, that's the moment God stops blessing and His favor evaporates from my life.

Here's an interesting Scripture when it comes to being content: "Now concerning spiritual gifts, brethren, I would not have you ignorant" (1 Cor 12:1 KJV).

Have you ever heard anyone singing in a microphone and thought: *They should not be singing?* Let's face it: There are some people who have no business singing and leading others in worship at church. It's not their gift. Yet for some reason, many don't get the hint. They try and they try to get up in front of people and show their so-called talent to the body. When all along, they've not come to terms with the fact God never intended them to be used in this type of ministry.

"God also testified to it [salvation] by signs, wonders and various miracles, and gifts of the Holy Spirit distributed according to His will" (Heb 2:4). This verse clearly shows us that God has distributed gifts throughout the body of Christ according to His choosing. And I'm sorry to say, but you cannot choose the gift God has blessed you with. He knit you together in your mother's womb. He knows the number of hairs on your head. He knows you better than you know yourself. That same God distributed your gifts according to *His* will before you were even born.

Paul's description of the body of Christ (the Church) is so invaluable:

> *Now there are diversities of gifts, but the same Spirit...For the body is not one member, but many. If the foot shall say, Because I am not the hand, I am not of the body; is it therefore not of the body? And if the ear shall say, Because I am not the eye, I am not of the body; is it therefore not of the body? If the whole body were an eye, where would be the hearing? If the whole were hearing, where would be the smelling? But now hath God set the members every one of them in the body, as it hath pleased Him. (1 Cor 12:4, 14-18 KJV)*

It's not important what part of the body you are. What's important is that you fulfill the task God has called you to. So what if you don't sing on the stage? So what if you don't preach? As long as you fulfill God's will—you stand on the same plane as the most well-known ministers in the world.

Ask yourself this question: *What part of the body has God created me to be?* I'm not asking what part you would like to be. I'm asking: What did God intend you to be before the ages of time?

If you don't know what your spiritual gifts are, I encourage you to take a Spiritual Gifts Test to help you identify some areas of gifting that you can seek the Lord about. Once you find out your place in the body, perhaps you might need to pray for contentment like Paul did.

God will strengthen you to be content with *your* spiritual gifts!

Success in Contentment

The choir has long been a place to help people develop their voices, as well as teach and inspire the church to worship. Sheila was probably my most faithful choir member and had a deep desire to sing on the worship team. Every time auditions were opened, she'd practice harder than anyone. She knew every note of the song perfectly and could sing it in her sleep. Yet, after the audition, someone else would always end up on the team. I knew it really bothered her, but I was commissioned by my pastor to put our best foot forward when it came to selecting singers.

One night, I remember Sheila came into rehearsal looking a little pale. The first half hour of choir practice, we dedicated to spending time in God's presence. On this particular night, God showed up in a powerful and unusual way. Mid-song I felt impressed that someone needed to share something, so I stopped and asked. Sheila raised her hand and said: "I'm the one you're talking about. I've been sick with laryngitis all week." She began crying, "I've been bitter because I've never been able to sing in front. I love to worship God, but tonight God showed me what it is like not to be able to sing at all. When I was trying to sing—I couldn't. He told me not to worry about singing to anyone else except Him." By this time she was weeping. "Then I began to sing, and my voice came back, and I was able to worship Him again." I looked around the room and noticed several people wiping tears from their eyes.

Something broke in our worship ministry from that day on. I believe God used Sheila's testimony to break down the pride in many hearts. In the months to come, our church experienced a freedom in worship like we'd never experienced before. Why? Because people began to assume their proper positions in the body and be content in their spiritual gifts.

In the course of time, Sheila became my assistant. She never sang solos but became an active member of the worship team and helped me organize the entire worship ministry. What a blessing it is when we grow content with our spiritual gifts!

CHAPTER 10

Secret of Greatness

AT MOST FUNERALS I've attended, there's always a segment in which loved ones are encouraged to share stories about the deceased. Many times, family and friends will reenact events from the life of the deceased, portraying the unique character and personality of their loved one. Sometimes the stories are humorous. Sometimes they are serious. The intent is to honor the person for all he or she did to make the world a better place.

Every man and woman of God desiring to fulfill the Great Commission wants his or her life to mean something in the end. When it's all said and done, we all want to leave our mark on the world. Everybody, deep down, wants to make a difference in his or her circle of influence.

If I'm honest, I'd like to be like Abraham, remembered as a man of faith. Like David, I want to be remembered as a man after God's heart. Like Moses, I want to be remembered as a humble man.

We've discussed secrets in the heart of God throughout this book, addressing such things as being thankful, teachable, trusting, humble, etc. All these are good, dear secrets that please God's heart.

At my funeral, however, there's one thing I want more than people talking about my faith, patience, or humility. I want the room to be filled to capacity with those whose eternal destination was changed after meeting me. Let me sum it up like this: I want to be a great man!

I hear brakes squealing in my ears. *Wait a minute, Brian! I thought this was a book about discovering the secret heart of God. What's this about wanting to be great?* That thought beckons the question: Is it wrong to desire greatness?

Being the Greatest

During Jesus' earthly ministry, a squabble broke out among the disciples as to who was the greatest among them. Jesus rebuked them saying, "If any man desires to be first, the same shall be last of all, and servant of all" (Mark 9:35 KJV). You notice, in disgust He didn't tell them, "How dare you want to be great?" He didn't even say, "I don't want you to be great." In essence, He said, "If you want to be great, serve others more than yourselves."

There's nothing wrong with wanting to be a great man or woman, as long as you understand the meaning of greatness. In God's eyes, a great man or woman is someone who obeys His Word, acts with integrity, and serves others before himself or herself. As the disciples found out, greatness is not outdoing others or being better than everyone else. Greatness is not arriving at a particular position—CEO, president, world leader, celebrity, apostle, prophet, pastor, or even the Pope.

When my family stands around my casket, I hope they can look down at my body's empty shell and say, "Dad was a humble servant of God who was faithful and obedient to God's heart in his work as a husband, father, and minister of the Gospel." At that same moment, I could be standing before God Almighty. I want to be able to say, as the apostle Paul:

> *"I have fought the good fight, I have finished the race, I have kept the faith. Henceforth there is laid up for me the crown of righteousness, which the Lord, the righteous judge, will award to me on that Day, and not only to me but also to all who have loved his appearing." (2 Tim 4:6-8 RSV)*

That is greatness!

Maximum Effectiveness

I never chose a life of ministry. As a preacher's kid, I grew up around it. It was all I knew. And when I attended college, my aspirations were not for ministry but for music. Upon graduating, however, my father offered me my first ministry job, and I desperately wanted to turn it down. Having grown up around ministry, I knew how difficult it was and wanted to get a job outside the church. As I'm sure you've concluded, God had other plans. And after much prayer, I accepted the job.

Once I yielded to God's plan, things changed dramatically. I felt a passion for God I'd never experienced before. And, even though I was new to full time ministry, I found success in most everything I did.

Shortly after accepting the position as worship leader, I also began a college ministry, which was non-existent at my home church. I always wondered why the church did an adequate job ministering to youth and a horribly sub-par job ministering to young adults beyond high school. After realizing the need, I felt God tell me, "Do something about it." So, I did.

Around that same time, I also began praying a specific prayer on a consistent basis. I can't even remember where it came from, but I found myself praying it almost every day for a couple years: "God, help me to walk in maximum effectiveness for the Kingdom—no matter what that looks like." I didn't understand it completely but felt drawn to pray for it. And even though I didn't grasp it, I knew God understood what I meant. My desire was to be used by Him in the maximum capacity He saw fit.

After two years of praying this prayer, one day, I discovered a secret in the heart of God concerning what I'd been praying. After praying my usual prayer, God asked me: "Do you want to know what maximum effectiveness for the Kingdom looks like?"

I've been praying it for two years, I thought, and, of course, said, "Yes."

"Okay then," God replied, "Learn to reproduce yourself."

In this one statement, I knew He'd just altered the course of my life. I was no longer called to hold college services and lead times of worship. He was calling me to train others to fulfill *their* God-given destiny, just as I was doing.

I wonder if Paul felt a little apprehensive at first telling those around him, "Follow me as I follow Christ." (see 1 Cor 11:1). Yikes! What a statement. What a responsibility. And, even when God shared this secret of discipleship with me, it took some convincing before I was able to make such a statement.

Do you see the corner I was turning? It was easy preaching sermons from a platform without being actively involved in the lives of those I was preaching to. It was easy to plan and execute college services or lead worship times without actually creating any disciples. I was busy "doing ministry" but not personally reproducing myself in anyone.

The next week I stood in front of our college group with a lump in my throat, and told them what God had shared with me. "Our ministry is getting ready to change," I said. "No longer is my goal ministering to you, but I'm going to teach you how to minister." The blank stares and confused looks weren't very reassuring.

"I feel God is leading me to step alongside you and help you discover His destiny for your life. So, today is a new day. And, instead of coming to receive, I want everyone to start coming with a mindset of what do I have to offer God." I went on to promise them access to me personally and reassured them I was going to make it a point to be a part of their lives.

As I passionately shared my heart, their apprehension seemed to fade. I sensed they were still confused and wondered: *What is this going to look like?* But, I also sensed they were open to the idea. It was a shaky start, but it was a start.

The Outcome

Over the next decade, this change in approach led to significant results. I'd like to say our college ministry grew exponentially in a few years, but that wasn't the case. Over ten years, however, here's what I saw God do: The denomination I was a part of took notice of what we were doing and placed me in charge of developing young adult ministry with oversight of a hundred churches.

During those years, we launched several college groups in churches in our region and started an organization sending ministry teams out for weeks at a time. By the end of my tenure, we'd sent teams to Mexico, the Philippines, Honduras, El Salvador, and dozens of teams all over the continental United States. God honored His approach of empowering people to do ministry in a way I never thought possible.

Out of those tours, we also started a nine-month internship, leased and renovated a housing facility, hired two families as dorm parents, and, that first year, signed up eight students. The second year we had sixteen and the third year, twenty-two. Between the second and third year, fifteen interns signed up to take the Honduras/El Salvador mission trip. I'm still mesmerized by what God accomplished during that tour.

God-Sized Challenge

Looking towards the upcoming trip, I held a planning meeting to pray and prepare for our soon departure overseas. Before the meeting, I felt God's leading to throw out a God-sized challenge and told the team: "What if we prayed and believed that God would do something to impact Honduras and El Salvador while we're there? I'm not talking about a few orphanages blessed and some churches encouraged. I'm talking about praying, fasting, and believing that these two nations will never be the same because of our time there!"

I looked around the room and saw faith rising in the faces of each team member. We came into agreement and started praying, fasting, and preparing. By the time the trip came around, all of us felt we had built a faith that could move mountains.

On the trip, two things happened. First, in Honduras, the ministry we were partnering with received a phone call from the office of the nation's president and first lady, asking to see what they were doing to impact several orphanages in Tegucigalpa. The leader of that ministry told them they would be visiting several orphanages in the next few days.

Surprisingly, the office called back and informed them that the president and first lady wanted to attend. After the phone call, the leader of the ministry, Jimmy, came to me and said, "I need your team to help me show the president and his wife what we do. We are short-staffed, so can you join our team, still doing the presentations you've planned, and help us make an impression on them while they visit?"

We agreed, of course, and a few days later, presented all we'd practiced—dramas, music, and acts of service—in front of the president, his wife, and administration. About an hour and a half after their entourage arrived and watched what we were doing, the limos and security detail drove off. We were shocked and amazed—thankful God had allowed us to be used in such a capacity.

Secondly, the next week, we ministered at a youth conference in El Salvador. Our job was to train forty teams of young people to blitz San Salvador doing drama ministry. Over three days, we worked tirelessly at preparing them to hit the streets. On the last night, a concert was held in an amphitheater, and we ministered to over ten thousand people. It was an unbelievable event that far exceeded the expectations of the host ministry.

God-Sized Results

Through the years, every trip we took, both nationally and abroad, was followed up with a party and time of debriefing. These were held about a week after the trip was over. The day before the meeting, I received a startling phone call with some results from the trip. I barely slept that night and couldn't wait to share the good news the following morning.

It was great to see everyone well rested and ready to share testimonies, celebrate, and rejoice over the miracles we'd seen. I quieted the rambunctious group and told them I had some great news to share from the trip.

"Do you remember the challenge I made about believing God to make a lasting impact on the two nations we were visiting?"

Everyone shook their heads yes and seemed excited to hear the results.

"Yesterday I received a phone call," I continued, "and I couldn't believe what I heard on the other end of the line. I also received an e-mail early this morning with more good news. Do you want to know what happened?"

"Just tell us already," one of the young guys blurted.

"Okay, okay," I said. "First off, in Honduras, they received word back from the president's office. As you know, the government is very frustrated with the current state of many of their orphanages nationwide. They've been at a loss regarding what to do with their foster care system, but were so impressed by what they saw, they've decided to hand the keys to Jimmy and give his ministry oversight of every orphanage in the nation. They are giving his staff full reign as well as funding to improve every orphanage facility nationwide."

Every jaw fell open—utterly stunned, as I had been.

"He wanted me to thank you. He feels that your presence made the difference in receiving this breakthrough."

We couldn't believe it! Everyone rejoiced that our prayers had been answered. God had done it. He'd used us to make a monumental impact. But, I wasn't done yet.

"I also received word this morning about our time in El Salvador. And guess what? The cards were collected of those who made decisions for Christ after all the teams hit the streets. Do you want to know how many came in?" I asked.

Everyone held their breath during my dramatic pause.

"Over one-hundred thousand cards were collected and distributed to hundreds of churches in order to follow up on them!"

Since that summer, I've seen some miraculous things happen, but I've never seen such staggering results as what we experienced on that mission trip. And where did it begin? It started with one God-sized challenge to believe for God-sized results.

Thinking back to all God did on that trip, I can't help but reflect on the two years I prayed for maximum effectiveness for the Kingdom of God—no matter what that looked like. From the shaky start of recalibrating a typical college ministry to making the decision to reproduce myself in others, I'm utterly amazed at how God honored my efforts.

Two Kinds of Fruit

I believe greatness can be summed up in accomplishing two things: bearing much fruit and bearing fruit that remains (see John 15:8, 16). Arriving at that destination on the road to greatness doesn't happen overnight. I've learned it takes time.

Bill Gates made a great quote that applies to bearing significant fruit:

"We always overestimate the change that will occur in the next two years and underestimate the change that will occur in the next ten."[14]

It appears God plays the spiritual stock market and blesses those who do the hard work of investing in the few, not simply drawing crowds of onlookers.

Recently, I was invited to speak at the fifteen-year anniversary of the sending organization I founded. I spoke to three teams being sent out to two different states. I was excited to speak, but was also excited because my oldest daughter was a part of the team traveling to Arizona. When I took the microphone, I had a surreal moment, thinking back to our humble beginnings all those years ago. Now, many years removed, I scarcely recognized anyone. And yet, as I looked closer, I did see people I knew salt and peppered throughout the crowd.

At one point during my message, I asked, "How many of you were a part of the tours back when I was in charge?" Over a dozen scattered individuals stood to their feet. Almost all of them, now in leadership, were either significant members or interns of the college group when I was in charge. I couldn't help but grow emotional. Fifteen years later, they were still in ministry making an impact on the next generation. *When God's goals become our goals, greatness is accomplished: Much fruit and fruit that remains.*

CHAPTER 11

Secret of Diligent Faith

DISCOVERING THE SECRET heart of God is a lifelong journey. And yet, the secrets are accessible—fully available to all who dare to come to Him on His terms. David understood this and summarized God's deep desire to share His secrets with us:

> *Praise the Lord, my soul, and forget not all His benefits—who forgives all your sins and heals all your diseases, who redeems your life from the pit and crowns you with love and compassion, who satisfies your desires with good things so that your youth is renewed like the eagle's. (Ps 103:2-5)*

The secret heart of God is filled with outstanding benefits. They are available to those willing to take advantage of His promises. Check out this amazing list of secrets we've discussed so far:

- The secret of God's love for one—you
- The secret of blind trust in a trustworthy God

- The secret of learning from the mistakes of others
- The secret of humility through servanthood
- The secret of waiting on God
- The secret of receiving instruction
- The secret to usefulness
- The secret of thanking God for His blessings
- The secret of being content but not satisfied
- The secret of greatness by reproducing ourselves

What a glorious list of secrets in the heart of God. By humbling ourselves, we can crush Satan's secret of I and avoid his landmines of deception.

Access

As I meditate on the secret heart of God, I want to conclude with what is probably the most important secret of all. If you've been around church for any length of time, you've probably heard people quote this important passage, "And without faith it is impossible to please God" (Heb 11:6a). This Scripture is powerful and can appear disheartening at the same time. It also conveys an important truth.

It is possible to know all the attributes of the secret heart of God such as His love for one, humility, waiting, servanthood, and so on. But, without involving faith, you cannot access them. Ouch! *Is that depressing to anyone else but me?* I so want to please God, yet I find my faith faltering at times. Maybe you can relate.

Listen to the entire verse from above, not just the first half: "But without faith it is impossible to please Him: for he that cometh to God must believe that He is, and that He is a rewarder of them that diligently seek Him" (Heb 11:6). All of us have moments where our faith is weak. All of us doubt at times. The disciples certainly did. And yet, God used them to change the world. Why? God rewarded their diligence!

Diligence of Faith

I believe in healing. Many don't today, but I do. I have since I was young. And yet, I've wondered why I wasn't seeing miracles such as those in the book of Acts. Don't get me wrong. People have told me their back was healed or their headache was gone after I prayed for them. I took their word for it, and I thanked God for it. At the same time, I also wondered: *Why did God heal their back and not the person in the wheelchair or the one on crutches over there?*

I felt I had faith. In fact, I knew it. Through the years, I'd seen God perform other types of miracles such as financial breakthroughs, dreams coming to pass, and people with hardened hearts coming to know Christ. When it came to healing, however, it felt like there was a block.

I've recorded several worship albums over the years. After a break of over five years, one day I felt God tell me I'd be recording again. He also instructed me to start writing music because He was far from done with me in that arena.

This was a surprise to me. At the time, I was pastoring a small church plant and hadn't written any music for quite a while. I had no recording studio (as in other churches and ministries I'd worked), no money, and no venue to record.

Within six months' time, however, I had more than enough music and, what I felt, was some of the best songs I'd ever written. I also received a large donation from a church designated to create a new worship album. Lastly, I had another church open their venue to me for recording—as well as their worship community. All seemed to be falling into place. But there was still one small problem I failed to mention. Due to all the traveling, recording, and vocal ministry through the years, I had no voice. I knew something was wrong, and even in doing therapy, I was still struggling.

A few months later I found myself at a night of worship. I was actually serving at the event, running a video camera. Worship was done, and while receiving an offering, the speaker stopped and said, "I believe God wants to heal someone right now. I'm going to pray in a minute and, as I do, lay your hand on that part of your body and believe God for your healing."

Now remember, I'm the guy who has the block on the whole healing thing. I've seen breakthrough in every other area but that. And yet, as the man was talking, I felt like it was God speaking right to me. My heart was racing, my palms got sweaty, and all I could think about was: *My voice. God wants to heal my voice.*

The man prayed, and as he did, I laid my hand on my throat and said, "Lord, I receive Your healing right now." As I did, it felt like something on the inside turned a summersault, almost like God was cutting and attaching things. I knew it was a Holy surgery of my vocal cords.

When I arrived home that night, I immediately went to the piano to thank God. Within a few minutes of singing and worshiping, I realized my voice had been completely healed. With a heart of thanksgiving, I wrote this song:

Heart Strings

I, I have a voice to sing
You've given that to me
I, I have a song in my heart
You've given me one to sing
It's the music of my heartstrings
And it goes like this...
I thank you, I thank you
I thank you for being so good...to me

At church, the following Sunday, I shared what had happened and sang the song God had given me. My voice never felt better—stronger than it had been in years. As I worshiped, gratitude seemed to gush from my heart as I sang the words.

After the service, a woman came up to me and said, "God healed me when you were singing your song."

I was shocked and asked, "What did God heal you of?"

"My back was in terrible pain, as usual," she replied. "Now it feels completely better."

I was cordial and smiled, but I'm embarrassed to admit thinking: *Oh goodie, God healed her back. Here we go again. The block is back.*

As much as the thought plagued me, something inside couldn't accept that. My voice had been healed—legitimately healed. Instead of doubting, I held on to faith.

Halfway Around the World

A few summers later, I went to Africa on a mission trip. During my time in an impoverished area of Tanzania, I preached my heart out at a crusade. The Holy Spirit was so present. Here's my journal entry after that night:

August 22

After they dismissed the crowds, the people wouldn't leave. Instead, people started flooding the stage. I asked my interpreter what was going on and she said, "These people are sick and need healing."

Before long the stage was filled. I noticed a man struggling to stand, using a stick to hold himself up. He was skin and bones, and very sick I could tell. In my mind I had a split-second vision and saw myself kicking the stick out from underneath him. I immediately thought: "There's no way I'm doing that!" Before long, however, they led our prayer team down the line to lay hands on the sick. Before long, I found myself face to face with the crippled man. Instead of doing what I saw, I laid my hand on his head and, with as much faith as I could muster, said, "Be healed in Jesus' name!" Nothing happened. When he wasn't healed, I moved on to the next person.

When I reached the end of the line, the Holy Spirit told me, "You didn't obey me. Go back and do what I told you to do."

I was so scared, but had another thought: What if this man is not healed because of my disobedience. My heart was beating so fast, and I knew what I had to do, but I was afraid to do it. Finally, I made my way back to him, reared back and kicked the stick out from underneath him! It flew aside, and I heard the whole crowd gasp! Then it grew quiet. I felt the eyes of everyone looking at me—and at the man.

He wobbled a bit, and I was prepared to catch him if he fell. But, he didn't. Instead, he smiled at me. I looked down at his legs and saw them growing stronger. "Walk in Jesus' name! Walk!" He did and before long he was running up and down the stage—healed!

This wasn't the only healing I saw. During worship the following night, I had the same kind of split-second vision. I saw myself bopping someone on the ears with both hands. Even though I was again uncomfortable with God's command, I tucked it away and thought: *Okay God. If that's what you want me to do, I'll do it.*

August 23

The whole night transpired without incident. Just as we were getting ready to leave, I saw a group of pastors praying over someone. I walked over and saw the little girl they were praying for. When we made eye contact, she growled, and then screamed. I asked one of the pastor's what was wrong with her, and he said, "She's deaf." As soon as the words left his mouth, I knew this was the girl I was to pray for. And I also knew her condition was caused by a demonic spirit.

I knelt down and looked at her calmly. She was still screaming loudly. Then I raised my hands and bopped her forcefully on both ears. What I saw was astounding! She stopped screaming and her facial expression changed immediately. It was pleasant—calm. I noticed her dark black eyes turned a greenish blue color. Then she smiled at me. The demon was gone, and she could hear!

Since that trip to Africa, I've seen more miracles than at any other time in my twenty years of ministry. What was the secret of God's heart I learned? Be diligent in your faith and don't quit. As we read earlier, although without faith it is impossible to please Him, the opposite is also true: *with faith, it is possible to please Him.* He is the "rewarder of those who diligently seek Him" (Heb 11:6).

The secret of diligent faith will unleash all the secrets I've mentioned throughout this book, allowing God to restore every dream according to His plan in His time.

Even when your faith feels small and doubt tries to creep in—keep believing! When you don't understand what He's doing—keep believing! When you find yourself at the Red Sea and Pharaoh's army is closing in—keep believing! When your dreams are delayed—keep believing! When a loved one is sick and dying and you experience disappointment such as Mary and Martha did—keep believing!

Within the secret heart of God, His promises are waiting. By faith, lay hold of them!

References

1. Cook, Amanda and Gretzinger, Steffany. *Brave New World.* "Pieces," Bethel Music Publishing, 2015. All Rights Reserved. Used by Permission.
2. Scataglini, Sergio. *The Fire of His Holiness: Prepare Yourself to Enter into God's Presence, 2nd edition.* Worldwide Publishing Group, 2014.
3. Warren, Rick. *The Purpose Driven Life: What on Earth Am I Here For? Expanded edition.* Grand Rapids: Zondervan, 2013.
4. John Musker, et al. *Aladdin*. (Burbank, CA: Walt Disney Pictures, 1992),
5. The Essence of Quotations; "Amazing Otto von Bismarck Quotes: What He Said or Not," https://www.quotesandsay ings.com/general/amazing-things-otto-von-bismarck-said-or-not/ accessed August 2017.
6. Kent, Dan G. *The Layman's Bible Book Commentary (Book 4).* Baptist Sunday School Board, 1980.
7. Lotz, Anne Graham. "Nobody's Hopeless" 2013 Decision Magazine
8. DoesGodExist.org; "Abraham Lincoln: Often a Failure," http://www. doesgodexist.org/JanFeb04/AbrahamLincoln OftenAFailure.html accessed August 2017.
9. Chapman, Elvin S. *Latest Light on Abraham Lincoln and Wartime Memories.* Fleming H. Revell Company, 1917.

10.Weber, Stu. *Tender Warrior: New Edition.* Multnomah, 2006

11.Nance, Terry. *God's Armor Bearer, Revised edition.* Spirit Filled Books, 2003.

12.Forbes.com; "St. Bernard," https://www.forbes.com/quotes/theme/humble/ accessed August 2017.

13."That's Life" by Vernon Duke, E. Y. Harburg © Warner/Chappell Music, Inc., Universal Music Publishing Group, Imagem Music INC, Shapiro Bernstein & Co. INC.

14.BrainyQuote.com; "Quotes Bill Gates," https://www.brainyquote.com/quotes/quotes/b/billgates404193.html, accessed August 2017.

ABOUT THE AUTHOR

Brian Ming started writing songs and poems at age sixteen. His love for writing music led to authoring fiction, often coupling songs with storytelling. His first novel and public debut, *Snow Sometimes Falls*, received rave reviews and quickly became an Amazon Bestseller. He is also the author of several short stories, the *Future Kingdom Series,* and the *Secret Heart Series*.

Brian is a speaker, author, songwriter, and worship leader whose passion to teach others how to develop their God-given creativity to the fullest has inspired many. He currently resides with his wife Kristen and their three children in Fontana, California.

More info on the latest books, stories, and music:
www.brianandkristenming.com

Made in the USA
San Bernardino, CA
25 August 2017